GOOD ENOUGH TO BE GREAT

GOOD ENOUGH TO BE GREAT

The Inside Story of Maryland Basketball's National Championship Season

Josh Barr

Since 1947
REGNERY PUBLISHING, INC.
An Eagle Publishing Company • Washington, DC

Library of Congress Cataloging-in-Publication Data

Barr, Josh.
Good enough to be great : the inside story of Maryland basketball's national championship season / Josh Barr.
p. cm.
Includes index.
ISBN 0-89526-115-4
1. University of Maryland at College Park—Basketball. 2. Maryland Terrapins (Basketball team) 3. NCAA Basketball Tournament. I. Title.
GV885.43.U535 B37 2003
796.323'63'0975251—dc21
2002154524

Published in the United States by
Regnery Publishing, Inc.
An Eagle Publishing Company
One Massachusetts Avenue, NW
Washington, DC 20001

Visit us at www.regnery.com

Distributed to the trade by
National Book Network
4720-A Boston Way
Lanham, MD 20706

Printed on acid-free paper
Manufactured in the United States of America

10 9 8 7 6 5 4 3 2 1

To Jodi, who gets it

CONTENTS

FOREWORD
by Michael Wilbon

It's a basketball school, without doubt, yet had it no validation. There was never a banner flying from the arched ceiling of Cole Field House, not the right kind anyway. Sure, there were jerseys of All-Americans like Tom McMillen and John Lucas, even Gene Shue. But for all the great players like Buck Williams and Len Bias, for all the memorable ACC battles, particularly through the 1970s and 1980s, for all the promises like the one Lefty Driesell once uttered, that Maryland would become the "UCLA of the East," the University of Maryland had no basketball history worth celebrating unconditionally.

There was always something either unlucky or inadequate about Maryland basketball. There was no national championship when the twentieth century ended; there were no trips to the Final Four, only one trip to the regional finals in all those years, with all those great players. Okay, most schools never get a sniff of the Final Four; there are plenty of schools of Maryland's size and with its resources who would trade basketball histories with Maryland in a second. Problem is, Maryland's campus sits between two impassioned basketball cities, Baltimore and D.C., also two of the most fertile recruiting grounds in America. Also,

Maryland is a charter member of a conference that between 1982 and 1999 sent five schools—North Carolina, North Carolina State, Duke, Virginia, and Georgia Tech—to the Final Four, but not Maryland. The Terrapins always seemed to be the poor relations, or better yet, Wile E. Coyote, scheming and plotting to the best of their ability but always beaten by the Tar Heel or the Blue Devil.

The greatest basketball game in ACC history? Everybody knows it was N.C. State's overtime victory over Maryland in the conference tournament title game in 1974 that propelled N.C. State to the national championship and Maryland, well, home, since back then a conference could send only one representative to the Big Dance. Nobody seemed to suffer more gut-wrenching losses than Maryland. There was the Steve Francis–led team losing to St. John's in 1999 when a run to the Final Four had seemed possible. There was the thirty-five-point loss to UCLA in 2000; it's possible a good team with experienced players has never been so thoroughly dominated. There was the thirty-five-point blowout loss to Bob Knight and Indiana back in 1981, made all the worse because Georgetown the next year would make the Final Four for the first of three trips in four seasons. Has a charter ACC team ever been the number-two college team in its own market?

Then, of course, the death of Len Bias, the tenure of Bob Wade, subsequent NCAA probation, and the stunningly excessive and cowardly sanctions handed down that were all too close to the death penalty—all of it made just reaching the tournament again a triumph.

I was the *Washington Post*'s beat writer covering Maryland basketball for the 1981–82, 1982–83, and 1983–84 seasons. Buck Williams had just left school after his junior year for the NBA, and the program was transitioning from the Williams–Albert King–Ernie Graham era to that of Adrian Branch and Bias, the team that would give Lefty Driesell his only ACC tournament championship, in 1984. None of us suspected at the time that Driesell would be pretty much out of magic moments at Maryland. It's amusing to look back now and recall how Driesell was hailed as a great recruiter but not much of a bench coach, when in fact Driesell virtually never won recruiting battles with North Carolina's Dean Smith or Duke's Mike Krzyzewski. There was nothing quite like Driesell railing against the referees, or for that matter against the basketball gods after a loss to North Carolina or Virginia. Twenty years later, it's Driesell's resilience I most admire and that proved to be the logs that kept the fire burning inside the program.

In fact, it's that resilience, along with the outward passion, that connects Driesell and Gary Williams. After the NCAA imposed crippling sanctions on Maryland in 1990, the program needed not only a veteran coach but also a sustained infusion of energy and a commitment that went far beyond the professional. Gary Williams, an alum whose passion has always bordered on the maniacal (at least on the bench), was uniquely qualified. This wasn't a job; it was closer to a calling. Had Williams left, it probably would have set Maryland back years. Instead, Williams stayed, and he recruited a freshman named Joe Smith who helped beat Georgetown and make Maryland the number-one local attraction again for the first time in more than ten years. Maryland got into the tournament and beat John Calipari and UMass. Keith Booth arrived, and then Steve Francis, if only for one year. Williams had his alma mater back on the national radar.

It's completely appropriate that Maryland should reach its first Final Four after that January 2001 collapse at home against Duke. The Terrapins' signature under Williams is that they play better when trailing, better when challenged publicly, better when the underdog. The best thing going for Maryland in 2001, besides a deep and diversely talented roster with a special player in Juan Dixon, was having to play so many favored teams along the way.

The same principle applied in 2002, when Maryland had to defeat Kentucky, Connecticut, Kansas, and Indiana en route to a national championship. There were no shortcuts there. All the Terrapins had to do along the way was defeat four schools that had won national championships in the past fifteen years, four schools that help make up college basketball royalty, four schools that have plenty of banners hanging from the ceilings of their gymnasiums. And in beating them, Maryland not only won a national championship, but the program at last had validation for all the previously unrewarded effort put forth by so many players and coaches, those who came close, and those who didn't.

The Terrapins' perseverance and talent finally allowed the writing of a happy ending for Maryland basketball, and now Josh Barr, my colleague at the *Washington Post,* is here to tell the whole story. Nobody knew this team better than Josh, who has been on the Maryland basketball beat for four years. He knows the story inside and out. And it's an amazing story.

GOOD ENOUGH TO BE GREAT

PROLOGUE

No Ordinary Season

Juan Dixon had made this drive on plenty of other nights.

It was a routine of sorts. A team manager would leave the lights on at the University of Maryland's arena, Cole Field House, and Dixon could have the place all to himself to shoot, dribble, clear his mind, and think about what lay ahead in Maryland's next game.

This night was different, however. Coaches and players like to say that they treat every game the same, but less than forty-eight hours away lay a game like no other. The opponent was Duke, the team Maryland's students loathed and its players looked to as the team to beat in the chase for a national title. Beat Duke, and anything would be possible. After all, the Blue Devils were the defending national champions and had spent all but one week this season atop the national polls.

And no one, it seemed, relished the challenge more than Dixon. In just a few years, he had come further, perhaps, than anybody. Now a senior, he had been a virtual nobody as a high school recruit; news that he had accepted a scholarship offer from Coach Gary Williams had been greeted with a less-than-overwhelming response from Maryland fans.

Why, many had wondered, did Williams want this skinny kid from Baltimore who could do nothing but shoot?

During the course of his career at Maryland, though, Dixon had transformed himself into one of the nation's elite college players. He might have lacked some of the physical tools that made many top collegians think they were ready for the NBA after just a season or two, but Dixon more than made up for that with his savvy and determination. Playing in one of the country's premier conferences, the Atlantic Coast Conference (ACC), he had been named first-team All-ACC as a sophomore and a junior and soon would be named to the team again as a senior.

While much of College Park was preening for the Friday-night scene, Dixon was in Cole Field House's home-team locker room, sitting in his stall on the left side. He put on his practice jersey—the same number 3 he had worn so many times—and the practice shorts, the ones with the letters "RWIT" (Remember What It Takes) stitched in white in the back, and he laced up his shoes.

This was a part of the game that Dixon enjoyed. Getting in the gym for a few extra hours, working on a certain aspect of his game, imagining what the upcoming contest might be like.

Unlike many college students, most of Maryland's basketball players were not much for partying. They preferred playing video games and watching basketball on television to hitting the bars and being the center of attention. Dixon especially enjoyed the peacefulness of the apartment he shared with two teammates and a team manager.

Perhaps the only place Dixon felt more comfortable than in the apartment was on a basketball court. Ever competitive, he thrived on almost any kind of game. It didn't matter if it was a pickup game, a game of H-O-R-S-E (like the team had played the previous season to try to break the monotony of a near-disastrous stretch), or a half-court shooting contest (usually won by one of Dixon's roommates, Drew Nicholas).

On this night in mid-February, though, Dixon was nearly alone. As he walked out the tunnel from the locker room to the court, the forty-seven-year-old building was silent except for the thud of the Nike basketball he dribbled. The students who had camped out for two days to get tickets had already been rewarded with their ducats and surely were out enjoying the night. Now the only other people in Cole aside from Dixon were the few campus policemen who had been assigned the glorious task of preventing people from sneaking into the arena some forty hours before tip-off—which wouldn't be out of the question for a game of this magnitude, since the seats in Cole's student section were first come, first served.

Even without an audience, Juan Dixon was focused. As focused as he would be one month later in the NCAA tournament, when he would raise his game to another level and lead Maryland to its first national championship. It was this work ethic that had made him a special player in college, transforming him from a middling recruit into the ACC player of the year and the leading scorer in Maryland history.

Tonight, Dixon worked on his jump shot and imagined what it would be like in a day and a half, when the rival Duke Blue Devils made their annual trip to Cole. He broke a good sweat, then turned out the lights and went back to his apartment.

• • •

A few hours after Dixon fell asleep, the phone rang at Gary Williams's house.

When the telephone rings in the middle of the night, it almost never is a good thing. Good news can wait until a few hours after the sun rises; bad news never waits. Williams sensed two possibilities: either one of the players had gotten into trouble, which would have been surprising given the team's personality and the looming game against Duke, or something had gone wrong with his father, who had been hospitalized that week because of a virus.

When Williams heard the voice of his older brother, Douglas, on the other end of the line, he knew what was coming: their father, William Williams, had passed away at age eighty-five.

Within a few minutes, Gary Williams, ever the coach, had formed his game plan. Before Saturday's practice, he would tell a few close friends and his assistant coaches, doing so not to ask for support but merely to inform them of his situation.

"I knew it was something I had to handle myself," Williams said later. "You felt bad and all that, but at the same time, I've dealt with a lot of things by myself. So I was used to doing that. Just the idea, you don't want it to sound cold, but I knew the team had to be focused and I didn't want to disrupt the focus of the team. There was nothing they could do anyway."

Dealing with tragedy had become a theme for this team. Dixon's story was well chronicled, with both of his parents dying from drug-related AIDS while he was in high school. Assistant coach Dave Dickerson's father had passed away just before the season started. And in early December, forward Byron Mouton had returned home to Rayne, Louisiana, to bury an older brother who had been gunned down by an unknown assailant in Houston.

Still, no matter how accustomed the team was to heartbreak, on the eve of the game Williams did not want to burden his players with the news. They already had enough on their minds, with perhaps the biggest game of the season looming.

After a few hours of sleep, Williams was in the office early that Saturday morning, following his normal routine for a Sunday game. He relished the quiet of a weekend; with the team ranked third in the nation at 21–3 and the Duke game approaching, he had spent much of his week fielding phone calls from friends, colleagues, and members of the media. Now he had a little extra time to try to figure how the Terrapins could be successful against the nation's top-ranked team.

• • •

For any team, when Duke is the opponent it is not an ordinary occasion. For Maryland, the game seemed like the Super Bowl. The teams' rivalry had become among the most heated in the nation, fueled by some spectacular games. The previous season had seen the teams play four times, with Maryland leading by at least ten points in each game and winning only once. There was the colossal collapse at Cole, when the Terrapins led by ten points in the final minute of regulation and lost. Even worse might have been the loss in the NCAA tournament semifinals, when Maryland led by twenty-two points and fell, 95–84; it was the largest lead ever blown in the Final Four.

There was also the teams' first meeting this season, on January 17, when there were thirty lead changes in the first twenty-three minutes before Duke pulled away for a 99–78 victory.

The rivalry had blossomed to the point that former Maryland star Steve Francis, now playing for the Houston Rockets, made sure he was in attendance. Francis had scored twenty-seven points while playing all forty-eight minutes of a 109–100 loss to the Orlando Magic on Saturday night, but he looked as fresh as could be on Sunday when he spoke to the team in the locker room before the game.

This would be Maryland's only national network TV game of the season, something that was not lost on Williams, who seemed always to be fighting for attention in the ACC, a league dominated by Duke and North Carolina for much of its forty-nine-year existence.

On this day, though, the dominating was done by Maryland. Officially, there was one lead change, when Dixon drove from the left side and made a high-arcing scoop shot to make it 2–0 less than twenty seconds in. After that, it was almost all Maryland, with the Terrapins building a twenty-five-point lead and Francis playing the role of head cheerleader from the bench.

Chris Wilcox, the talented but inexperienced power forward, played his best game to date, with twenty-three points and eleven rebounds, thoroughly outplaying Duke standout Mike Dunleavy at both ends of the court. Until then, Wilcox had been relatively anonymous on the national scene, known only for possessing phenomenal athletic ability for a man standing 6 foot 10. In this game, though, which included five of the twenty finalists (Wilcox was not one of them) for the Naismith Award, given to the national player of the year, Wilcox was the star, beginning his march to becoming a top NBA draft pick.

It hardly mattered when Wilcox bricked a powerful one-handed dunk midway through the second half. "My bad," Wilcox mouthed in the direction of Williams, though it was difficult for both to keep from grinning.

The final score was third-ranked Maryland 87, top-ranked Duke 73.

In the locker room afterward—after the students had mobbed the court and the extra-heavy security force had had to protect Duke's team and fans—Maryland's players were ecstatic.

They could envision two more meetings with the Blue Devils—just as in the previous season, when the teams played in the ACC and NCAA tournaments. But the Terrapins' domination on this day had been so complete that they had reason to believe they truly were a national championship contender, maybe even a favorite. On so many other occasions, Maryland had been close to this level, only to see something go awry at the last minute. Now first place in the ACC—and so much more—was firmly within the Terrapins' reach.

Keep playing like this, the players sensed as they waited for Williams to make it to the locker room, and they could be standing on the Georgia Dome court on April 2, celebrating the team's first national title.

Just another game. Just another season.

Yeah, right.

CHAPTER 1

Only One Goal

Steve Blake had gone out to dinner, wanting to think about anything but basketball. But there was a television in the restaurant, and since Blake admits that his life revolves around basketball, well, he had to catch a few glimpses. When he got home, he caught part of the second half, as Duke beat Arizona for the 2001 national championship.

Quickly, he changed the channel to avoid watching the rival Blue Devils—the team Maryland's players, fans, and students loathed more than anything in the world—dance all over the court, hugging one another and then, one by one, snipping down the net.

"I didn't want to watch the game," Blake said. "I was so mad."

Blake wasn't alone. His Maryland teammates felt much of the same anger and pain, and so did their fans. The Terrapins had come so tantalizingly close during the 2001 season. In their minds, they were just as good as—if not better than—those Blue Devils.

But once again, Maryland could not pull it off when it mattered most, blowing a twenty-two-point lead against Duke in the NCAA tournament semifinals.

Another season without a championship. Another season that ended with a loss.

It would not be a big deal, except for how close the Terrapins had been. Only one team gets to go out with a victory. The others dream about what might have been; the better ones think about how one shot, one free throw, one close call could have made the difference. Maryland surely was among that last group. Indeed, the Terrapins had seemed well on their way to running Duke out of Minneapolis's Metrodome; they had been close enough to start thinking about playing in the season's final game, on a Monday night with everyone watching and a few thousand flashbulbs going off at the opening tip.

The Terrapins had played so unbelievably well, building a 39–17 lead over Duke in less than fourteen minutes, prompting Blue Devils coach Mike Krzyzewski to scream at his players for playing so poorly. There was nothing to lose; what were they going to do, lose by forty? It couldn't have gotten any worse for Duke or any better for Maryland.

Courtside, one newspaper reporter had written the top of his story, convinced that the outcome was decided. After all, no team had built such a considerable lead and lost at this late stage of the season.

"Left, right. Left, right. Duke fell to the canvas before knowing what hit it."

Of course, those words never saw print. The delete key came in handy for many reporters when Maryland lost the lead, and lost the game.

The Terrapins headed home the following morning still smarting. Being so close, Maryland's players could begin sensing what winning a national championship would be like.

And that made the hurt sting a little more.

Everyone, it seemed, replayed the game in his mind more than a few times the ensuing summer. Over time the anger faded, replaced with the annual hope that this would be Maryland's year. Many college basketball players share that hope in the summer and fall, but most have a better shot at winning the lottery. In reality, only a few teams in any given year have a realistic chance of winning the title.

During summer pickup games and individual workouts, the Maryland Terrapins started to think they weren't just better than a long shot but were in fact one of the favorites.

And why not? Maryland had lost only one starter off the team that had come so close to reaching the championship game. Juan Dixon, Lonny Baxter, and Steve Blake each had started for two years, and senior Byron Mouton was another returning starter. The only seniors on the 2000–01 team had been Terence Morris, Mike Mardesich, and LaRon Cephas, and while Morris and Mardesich had played significant roles and the well-liked Cephas had been regarded as a team leader, none of the three was considered irreplaceable. Indeed, juniors Tahj Holden and Drew Nicholas had considerable experience and were expected to step up, and Chris Wilcox, though just a sophomore, had the potential to be a superstar, a player with amazing athleticism for someone who was 6 foot 10. The only other notable departure was that of forward Danny Miller, who had decided to transfer to Notre Dame for his senior season, but with Mouton, Maryland was still solid at the small forward position.

The Terrapins had lost longtime assistant coach Billy Hahn, Williams's top aide since 1989, who had taken the head coaching job at La Salle. The transition was relatively seamless, though, as assistants Dave Dickerson and Jimmy Patsos moved one slot up the flowchart and former Maryland guard Matt Kovarik got his first coaching job.

In all, the Terrapins had every reason to be confident. Everyone sensed it, from Dixon, the standout, to the last player on the bench, senior walk-on Earl Badu, to Gary Williams, the coach who had resurrected the once-troubled program.

"Obviously, people knew we had it all coming back, and everyone knew how good Chris was," Nicholas said. "Everyone on the outside couldn't really see it happening, didn't see it before the season started. . . .

Everyone was asking around, asking who was going to replace Terence [Morris] from the Final Four team. We were looking at Chris. He's a much different player, but we knew what he brought to the table for us."

The anticipation bubbled in the locker room, where players talked excitedly about making it to the Georgia Dome, site of the 2002 Final Four. And on a Friday night in mid-October, the players began to gather around 10 P.M. for the official start of the season, at midnight.

• • •

Midnight Madness is not so much about basketball as it is a chance for fans to get a glimpse of that season's players—to see what the newcomers look like and to catch a few highlight-worthy dunks. The real basketball starts the next morning.

Still, it was a festive atmosphere that night in Cole Field House. Some folks were beginning to grow nostalgic, aware that this would be the final season played in Cole, with the shiny $107 million Comcast Center—with air-conditioning and far more than four bathrooms—set to be the Terrapins' home for the 2002–03 season. Others were reveling in the school's athletic success. The basketball team was a perennial power, having been invited to eight consecutive NCAA tournaments. Now the Terrapins also were a hit on the football field, something the university hadn't seen for nearly two decades.

In fact, when Maryland's basketball team had won at Duke during the 1999–2000 season, jubilant students had torn down the goalposts in Byrd Stadium and carried them across campus to Fraternity Row. Told of this that night, one North Carolina sportswriter had joked, "Well, they probably were the oldest goalposts in the ACC."

He was probably right.

But Maryland's football team, under first-year coach Ralph Friedgen, was no longer a laughing matter. The previous night, the team had pulled out a stunning 20–17 overtime victory at Georgia Tech, putting the Terrapins at 6–0 and making them eligible for their first bowl game since 1990.

When the football team was introduced at Midnight Madness, it received a raucous ovation. But the biggest noise was still to come, when just before midnight the men's basketball team was introduced.

The fan favorites were easy to identify. There was Wilcox with his spectacular dunking ability. There was Baxter, who had been voted the most outstanding player in the NCAA tournament's West Region the previous season.

And of course there was Dixon.

The skinny kid from Baltimore had lost both of his parents to AIDS while he was in high school, and most observers had said he would never make it in the competitive Atlantic Coast Conference. Then he failed to meet the NCAA's minimum academic standards for freshman eligibility. When he achieved a passing score on the Scholastic Assessment Test (SAT), the Educational Testing Service, which administers the SAT, disqualified his score—apparently it had improved too much from that of his previous attempt. So Dixon took the test again. And passed again.

At Maryland, Dixon continued to beat the skeptics. He did it quietly. After all, he had to put some effort into dunking, and midrange jumpers aren't usually appreciated by the casual fan or the folks at ESPN cutting the *SportsCenter* highlights. Still, Dixon was named first-team All-ACC as a sophomore and as a junior, and was well on his way to establishing himself as one of the best basketball players ever in College Park.

Among those who identified with Dixon was Gary Williams, now entering his thirteenth season coaching at his alma mater. Both came from difficult family backgrounds and used basketball as a way to escape. On the court, there were no problems; when you stepped between the lines, the game was all that mattered, Williams often said. The two were fighters, having had to battle for nearly everything they had achieved.

Now Williams and Dixon hoped to use the game, their game, to take their school to new heights. For years, Maryland had always been just good enough to be good, but never great. Duke and North Carolina always seemed to be in the way, and even when Maryland could get past those two, something else would go wrong.

Perhaps the best team in school history was the 1973–74 squad, led by stalwarts Len Elmore, Tom McMillen, and John Lucas. That team didn't even play in the postseason, however. In those days, only one team from each conference qualified for the NCAA tournament. The winner of the ACC tournament represented the league in the NCAAs, and in the championship game North Carolina State edged Maryland in overtime, 103–100, in what is regarded as one of the greatest college basketball games ever played. While Maryland's players stayed in College Park, the Wolfpack, led by forward David Thompson—whom most observers still consider the greatest player in ACC history—went on to win the NCAA title, ending UCLA's unthinkable seven-year run as national champs.

Speaking of that 1973–74 Terrapin team, Williams said, "They were good enough to win the national championship. . . . That game [the ACC tournament final] was like the first game of the NCAA tournament. Play a bad game and you go home in the playoffs. They played a good game. And that still wasn't good enough."

Before the following season, the NCAA would enact new legislation to expand its tournament field: more than one team per conference could now be invited. For Maryland, though, it was one season too late. The Terrapins never lost by more than nine points in the 1973–74 season and finished 23–5, but what is remembered most is the loss to N.C. State.

The following season, 1974–75, with the multiple-team rule in place, Maryland made it to the NCAA tournament. In a field of thirty-two teams, all it took was two victories and the Terrapins were in the regional finals, one of eight teams left standing after they eliminated Creighton and Notre Dame. But a 96–82 loss to Louisville ended what was the most successful postseason in school history until the 2001 Final Four run.

In between, there were plenty of winning seasons but few major accomplishments. The most noteworthy events were a pair of disgraceful scandals that rocked the program in the 1980s.

The first came in 1986, when All-American Len Bias died of a cocaine overdose just two days after being selected second overall in the NBA draft by the Boston Celtics. After seventeen years coaching at the school, Lefty Driesell soon was ousted.

Driesell's successor, Bob Wade, landed the school in trouble with the NCAA for a variety of offenses, and within three years he was gone.

"I was never proud of my college career here at Maryland," said Maryland assistant coach Dave Dickerson, who played for the Terrapins from 1985 to 1989. "I wasn't proud of anything about it. The thing I was proud about was I got my degree."

Despite playing on two teams that advanced to the second round of the NCAA tournament, Dickerson said that unpleasant things came first to his mind when he thought of his playing days.

"The Len Bias thing," he said. "I was right in the middle of that. A nineteen-year-old kid. At the hospital that morning when they pronounced him dead. That sticks out in my mind. The other thing is just playing three years while Bob Wade was the head coach. There was no support, no love. There was always something going on, always someone transferring. I have negative thoughts about my four years playing, even though I played in two NCAA tournaments. Those things were short-lived, because as soon as you got home, something was going on. After my junior year, [standout freshman] Brian Williams transferred. A couple guys had academic issues."

Dickerson completed his eligibility the year before Gary Williams arrived, but he still was finishing up his degree during the 1989–90 season, Williams's first in the corner office of Cole Field House.

Had he known what lay ahead, Williams has said, he probably never would have taken the job. The NCAA came down with a sentence as harsh as had ever been handed out in basketball. Near the end of that first season, Williams learned that he would have to deal with scholarship and recruiting restrictions, that the team had been banned from postseason play for two years, and that Maryland had been prohibited from appearing on live television for the 1990–91 season. Since every game in the ACC tournament was televised, the Terrapins were barred from playing in that, too. And since that was the crown jewel that ACC athletic departments used to entice big-money boosters, Maryland was going to take a severe financial hit.

Indeed, there were some very dark days during which Williams wondered if he had committed professional suicide.

"I had doubts," Williams said. "It wasn't just not having enough good players. In fact, I had good players that first year. Jerrod Mustaf, Walt Williams, Tony Massenburg.... But they had been through so much, they had no spirit. It was like someone had taken the spirit out of them....

"We found out the week of the ACC [tournament] we were going to have sanctions the next three years. It was a very difficult thing for me, having never been through that before. And there were very negative feelings on campus toward the basketball program. It wasn't just getting the team to a point we could be competitive again, but getting people to believe we could be a positive thing for the school. It took a couple years to do that and then it took another year to get a good recruiting class after the sanctions."

Eventually, Williams built Maryland into a consistent winner. With an emerging star in then-freshman Joe Smith, who came out of high school as undistinguished as his name, the Terrapins made the NCAA tournament in 1994, winning two games and advancing to the Sweet Sixteen. They did it again in 1995 before being upended by a talented Connecticut team in the same round.

In 1998, with electric guard Steve Francis, Maryland was ranked as high as it had ever been, moving up to number two in the polls for a few weeks and earning a number-two seed in the NCAA tournament. But an upset loss to St. John's—and former George Washington coach Mike Jarvis—ended that run. The 1999 NCAA tournament ended with a Sweet Sixteen loss to a strong Arizona team, but 2000 closed with a disappointing blowout loss to UCLA in the second round.

The 2001 postseason run, though—even with the blown lead against Duke—buried the past. There was a victory over area rival Georgetown in the Round of Sixteen and then the victory over Stanford that put Maryland into the Final Four.

With that in mind, few in the Maryland community thought about the past disappointments, or even the Duke debacle, when looking ahead to the 2001–02 season. Undoubtedly, the rivalry with Duke was fierce, and the Terrapins recognized that many still wondered whether they measured up to the Blue Devils. Ultimately, though, Maryland had a much bigger goal in mind than simply avenging a loss from the previous season.

"We were so focused on what we had ahead of us," Steve Blake said, "that we never focused on what we had behind us."

Maryland was an experienced, talented, and confident team, so it was no wonder that Williams was relaxed that first night of practice, October 12.

Speaking in public, Williams normally is confident, comfortable with a microphone in his hand. The students in particular like his shtick after home games when the coach's postgame radio interview is broadcast in the arena. But when Williams took the microphone to address the crowd at Midnight Madness, it was no act as he boldly talked about the team's goals for the upcoming season.

"Last year we wanted to go to the Final Four," Williams said. "This year we want to win a national championship."

It was an unusual proclamation. Few coaches are willing to admit when they have great teams. Some, like football coach Lou Holtz, are notorious sandbaggers, refusing to acknowledge when they have a decent team. Everyone would prefer to be the underdog. There is less pressure that way. When the favorite wins, it is no big deal; but when the underdog wins, it is a great story. And no one wants to be the favorite that loses.

"I didn't know he was going to come out like that and say that," said Blake, who later in the season would deliver some of the year's more memorable quotes. "It was a bold prediction. But he believed it and we believed the same thing. We were just kind of shocked that he said it to everyone. Coaches like to keep that stuff in the locker room. There, we talk about winning the national championship and going undefeated. But you never say it [publicly]."

By the time Midnight Madness rolled around, however, Gary Williams had a good sense of what his team would be like. The players had been playing pickup games the past few months, and while NCAA rules prevented Williams and his staff from watching, reports had filtered back to the coaches.

While the trend in college basketball was for the best players to leave for the NBA after only one or two seasons, Maryland was an anomaly. The Terrapins would have three players in their third full season as starters: seniors Dixon and Baxter, and Blake, a junior. Mouton had started much of the previous season after transferring from Tulane, where he had started and led the team in scoring as a freshman and sophomore.

Perhaps the only key decision for Williams was at power forward, where Wilcox and Holden were battling for the starting role. The Terrapins also had a veteran reserve in Nicholas. That gave Williams seven players at his disposal, plus the possibility of using junior college transfer Ryan Randle (a center) or freshmen Mike Grinnon (a forward) and Andre Collins (a guard).

"We knew who our top seven players were," Williams said. "How many college basketball teams know that at that point?"

The team's belief that it was a national contender was bolstered when the preseason polls were released. Maryland was number two in the Associated Press media poll, as high as it had ever been, and number three in the ESPN/*USA Today* coaches poll. The team also had plenty of motivation, having come so close the previous season. Perhaps things finally were starting to line up for the Terrapins.

"We knew we were good enough and that we had guys who wanted to win a national championship. That was relaxing [in] itself," Dave Dickerson said. "First of all, to know you are good enough to win a national championship, that's a pretty damn good feeling as a coach. If things fall in place the right way, you can win. That's how I felt about this team [in August]. If we don't have any bad injuries or any unfortunate luck or something like that, then we're going to be one of those teams that could compete for a national championship.

"That was my standard line—there are about five to seven teams each year that can win the national championship. It's a great feeling to know you're one of those teams if things go right for you. I would talk to my family back in South Carolina. I would talk to Tony Massenburg and [former teammate and current Tiger Woods associate] Greg Nared about it. They felt the same way. And my wife and I talked about it a lot."

Fans also were talking about it. Once again, the team would be heavily scrutinized. Like it or not, many fans expected their beloved Terrapins, with such talent and experience, to win every game; any loss could be considered a catastrophe. And Williams knew it.

"Just to make the playoffs isn't good enough," Williams said. "What you have to do now is win. In football, if you make a bowl game, that usually is good enough. Where we are in basketball, now in the ACC, if you make the NCAA tournament, which has gotten harder to do, that's not good enough. And sometimes with the expectations, if you get to the Sweet Sixteen, that's not good enough either.

"This is a pro town. You have to accept that if you coach at Maryland. In a pro town and the nation's capital, everybody questions every policy. If the Republicans say something is good, the Democrats say it is bad. If the Democrats say something is good, the Republicans say it is bad. There is never a unanimous feeling about anything. And I really feel it carries over to sports around here. When things are going good and going your way up here, there are too many good things said about you. When things are going bad, there are too many bad things said about you. There are no normal situations."

Williams might have smiled at all the expectations for the Terrapins, knowing that, not all that long ago, many observers had sneered at his assortment of players.

CHAPTER 2

An Odd Collection

In college basketball, the saying goes, teams like Duke and North Carolina have rosters full of McDonald's All-Americans, while other schools' players only eat at McDonald's.

Maryland's recruits were always among those who only ate at the Golden Arches: their reputations carried little weight, and perhaps even slipped a notch, when they selected their college.

"It was ridiculous," Coach Gary Williams said. "You sign Juan Dixon, he's a bad recruit. You sign Lonny Baxter, he's a bad recruit. Drew Nicholas was not good enough; he wasn't good enough for the second guard position. I remember sitting in Cole Field House the year Keith Booth and Joe Smith played in that [high school] all-star game and people all around me—and it's an all-star game, so if you're not the point guard it's hard to look good—and people are saying those two guys aren't any good."

Smith would leave Maryland after two sensational seasons to become the number-one overall pick in the 1995 NBA draft. Booth stayed four years and was a first-round pick of the Chicago Bulls in 1997.

So maybe Williams recruited better than the pundits thought. Or maybe it shows just how inexact the recruiting process really is.

One look at Maryland's roster for the 2001–02 season revealed an odd collection of players. Some had been considered too short to play major college basketball. Others had been too soft. Only point guard Steve Blake had been seriously recruited by other top programs; he had opted for Maryland because it was almost guaranteed that he would be a starter from the day he walked on campus.

The others, though, had earned their way into their current positions. Dixon and Baxter were entrenched in their spots, having worked hard to shed their labels as undersized and not talented enough to play at this level. Sophomore Chris Wilcox, with his neatly braided hair, was beginning to display some flash and was competing with Tahj Holden to be the team's starting power forward.

And then there was the team's biggest character.

Byron Mouton.

From a small town in central Louisiana, Mouton had transferred from Tulane after two seasons there. He had to sit out the 1999–2000 basketball season, his first year at Maryland, to satisfy NCAA transfer rules, but he quickly made an impression on his new teammates. He was boisterous and funny, and made plenty of outlandish gestures, even in practice and pickup games. Sometimes he belly-flopped across the court. Other times he pumped a fist in the air or cupped his hands to his ears or did a handstand on the court.

Then there was the time in practice that he made a shot, jumped on a nearby team manager, and started riding him like a horse.

"Everybody took a look at this dude and thought he was on crack or something," Mouton said of himself. "What was wrong with him?"

Mouton's outgoing personality endeared him to teammates and classmates. It was rare for a night to pass without at least a few friends coming over to the Baltimore Hall suite he shared with three teammates to play video games or watch movies on the big-screen television. Mouton had quite a collection of games for PlayStation 2 and a host of DVDs from which to select.

"His room was like a movie theater," said teammate Calvin McCall, the former football quarterback who had accepted being a role player on the basketball team.

"Byron was interesting," Williams said with a chuckle. "Coming out of high school, he probably was as heavily recruited as any of our players. And he was Tulane's leading scorer his freshman and sophomore years. But I think Byron wanted to win. That was the most important thing to Byron. Byron was one of those people who was not upset to let you know how he is feeling—he was upset at Tulane, with the losing and their style. And that got some people upset at him, because he would show his dissatisfaction."

When Mouton decided to leave Tulane, he called one of his five brothers, Clyde, who lives in Waldorf, Maryland; Clyde helped put Mouton in contact with the Terrapins' coaching staff. Still, it was hardly a guarantee that Mouton would end up in College Park.

"We were a little concerned at first, because Byron didn't have a great reputation there," Williams said, admitting that he had had reservations about taking in a player who had made waves at his previous school.

In the end, though, Williams offered Mouton a scholarship and Mouton accepted it—or so Williams thought. When fall semester classes began that September, Mouton was nowhere to be found. He was supposed to be rooming with Holden, who at the time was a freshman. But Mouton was staying with his brother in Waldorf.

Mouton had grown up in Rayne, Louisiana, then headed a mere 150 miles west to go to Tulane. Now he was halfway across the country, in a place where he knew almost no one, and where he wouldn't be able to play basketball for another year. Mouton wanted to keep his options open a few days longer; once he started taking classes, he would be unable to transfer elsewhere. He was having serious second thoughts.

"Big-time," Mouton said. "I'm thinking I'm a long way from home. I didn't know how people were going to treat me, how I'm going to fit in. I'd never been that far from home."

Eventually, though, Mouton got over his homesickness. He felt challenged by assistant coach Dave Dickerson, who Mouton said called him a punk and told him to go home if that's what he wanted. Walk-on Matt Hahn, son of then–assistant coach Billy Hahn, helped show him around, and Mouton was surprised by how friendly his new teammates were.

And at least he could practice with the team. Whereas he had been frustrated with the Tulane program, he was thrilled to be playing with the Terrapins—and eager to show he belonged. Mouton set a personal goal to play so well in every practice that Coach Williams would yell at the starters for being outdone by someone from the scout team.

"Those were his games," Williams said, who was not surprised when told of Mouton's goal. "He was good. When the second team beats the first team, you do get mad, because they're supposed to be the good players. [Mouton] would laugh. He knew I'd go nuts."

Said Dave Dickerson, "He was probably the best player in the program that year he sat out. He did a hell of a job getting Coach to yell, because he was good and you couldn't stop him. He did it all over the court. It was almost like he had some type of awakening or divine intervention in his life where he fell in love with basketball all over again. He played the game with a zest you don't see every day."

The following season, 2000–01, Mouton shared time with junior Danny Miller—the only McDonald's All-American on the team—at small forward. But when Miller transferred to Notre Dame after the school year, Mouton was left unchallenged for the starting position.

• • •

With Mouton cemented at the 3, Maryland's rotation was nearly set. The ultracompetitive Blake and Dixon would start together in the backcourt for the third consecutive season. They weren't rated as highly as Duke's Jason Williams and Chris Duhon, but it would be difficult to find a more effective tandem. Baxter, who was as reserved as Mouton was gregarious, would start at center, also for the third consecutive season.

The only open spot was power forward, where Tahj Holden and Chris Wilcox would battle to replace Terence Morris.

Holden, who grew up on the Jersey shore, had shaken a reputation for being soft. He was somewhat beefy and not always smooth, but he had uncanny shooting range for someone who was 6 foot 10. During Maryland's run to the Final Four in 2001, Holden's three-pointer just before the halftime buzzer was a critical shot in the Terrapins' stunning 87–73 victory over top-seeded Stanford in the West Region final.

On campus, Holden was well respected. He was president of Maryland's Student-Athlete Advisory Council (SAAC) and vice president of the Atlantic Coast Conference's SAAC.

On the court, Holden had demonstrated enough ability that he was among the sixteen finalists for the twelve-player team that would represent the United States in the World University Games in China in August. But he had to withdraw from the final tryouts because of inflammation in his left foot.

"It was a hard decision," Holden said. "I really wanted to go. But it would not have been good to have two practices a day. Getting through one practice a day was tough enough."

Holden instead had to hear about the trip—and the problems finding suitable food—from Baxter and Dixon. Apparently, Chinese food in China is a little different from American Chinese food. While Baxter got sick from the food and Dixon joined other players desperately trying to find a McDonald's, Holden stayed home, visited with friends, and occasionally rode a stationary bike to stay in shape.

"You know how much fun that is," Holden said. "That's frustrating. You can't play basketball for two weeks. There is not much you can do."

While Holden was working his way back into shape, Wilcox just kept dunking away. Also 6-10, Wilcox had incredible athletic ability. He could jump and run like a guard, and he could do virtually anything on the court—save maybe shoot from the outside.

Athletic ability was the reason Maryland had plucked Wilcox from his high school in North Carolina. He had grown up in Whiteville, a town of five thousand in the southeastern part of the state, about thirty miles east of Lumberton off I-95; it's the kind of place where dirt roads and family cemeteries don't stick out.

As a youngster, Wilcox didn't stand out either. Though he was already 6-2 by the seventh grade, Wilcox was cut from the Chadbourn Middle School basketball team, which left a bitter feeling that remained for several years. "I was laid back because I just knew I had made the team," he said, remembering how on the first day of tryouts coaches measured the players' vertical jumps and he was unable to touch the rim. "But I walked in there and my name wasn't on that list. I went in the corner [of the locker room] and cried. All my boys had made it."

Wilcox kept playing basketball, though, and baseball, too. Sometimes he would leave baseball practice at Whiteville Park and run across the parking lot to the basketball courts to get in on the action there. Occasionally he would still be wearing cleats when he got on the court.

In eighth grade, Wilcox made the Chadbourn team and helped it go undefeated and win its league championship. That same year he made his first dunk, an event he still remembers vividly. He was in the Chadbourn Middle School gym with his godmother, helping to decorate for a school dance. They had finished their work and were on their way out the door, the lights off, when Wilcox decided to give it a try; he finally got the ball over the rim and through the net.

"I was psyched," he recalled years later, the fervor evident in his voice.

As a freshman at West Columbus High School, however, Wilcox did not make the varsity. In fact, when many of his junior varsity teammates were called up to the varsity for a holiday tournament, Wilcox was left behind. He still had a long way to go.

The following year, after transferring to Whiteville High, Wilcox began to emerge on the hardwood. His team advanced to the state semifinals before losing to a Wallace–Rose Hill team led by Ervin Murray, who was bound for Wake Forest. By that point, Wilcox was enough of a prospect that University of North Carolina coach Bill Guthridge made the two-hour trip to Whiteville to see him; the next year, Tar Heels assistant Phil Ford came to see Wilcox lead a team that eventually won the state championship.

But North Carolina's interest faded when it looked as if Wilcox would not meet the NCAA's minimum academic requirements to play as a freshman, since the ACC does not permit nonqualifiers to receive scholarships.

Maryland and North Carolina State continued to woo Wilcox, however. For his senior year, he moved to Raleigh to attend Enloe High, because an AAU coach thought that that school would better prepare him for the college boards. Each day, Wilcox and his mother, Debra Brown, picked a word out of the dictionary for him to learn. But other students wondered aloud if academics were the real reason that Wilcox came to Enloe; how much, they asked, were the coaches paying to bring in their new superstar? "I wish they were, so I could get some stuff out of it," Wilcox later said. "But that wasn't the case."

While schoolwork sometimes presented a difficulty, by this point basketball was easy for Wilcox. He was so much taller than his peers that he rarely had to work hard. His defensive assignment usually was to stand close to the basket and block shots; sometimes he didn't even have to leave his feet. And he almost never took a jump shot: teammates got him the ball in close for yet another rim-rattling, backboard-shaking dunk.

"I didn't like it when I saw him play because he never did anything," Gary Williams recalled. "But every once in a while, he did something that was ridiculous."

For that reason, Williams was willing to hold a scholarship for Wilcox as long as necessary in case the Enloe High star got a qualifying score on the SAT. North Carolina State, on the other hand, wanted Wilcox to go to prep school and could not wait to see if he would pass the test in time for the 2000–01 season. Maryland's decision to wait for Wilcox eventually made the difference.

As a freshman, Wilcox averaged just 8.6 minutes per game. When Maryland played at North Carolina, plenty of his friends and family made the short drive to be in attendance, but he didn't even get in the game. Since he was getting such limited playing time on a veteran team, some had difficulty gauging Wilcox's progress. To those around the team, however, it was apparent that he had made strides since the preseason, when he had struggled so badly that during one scrimmage he threw away four consecutive inbounds passes.

And the following summer, as most of the players remained around campus to take a few classes and work on their games, Wilcox's development became even more clear, particularly during the nightly pickup games at Cole Field House. In addition to current and former Maryland players, participants included some of the Washington Wizards' younger players and other NBA players with ties to the area.

"It just started to show," guard Drew Nicholas said. "He was going against Rodney White, who was the number-nine pick [in the first round of the 2001 NBA draft] and pretty much holding his own, playing all right. Guys were just kind of like, 'Wow.' And he looked a lot different than when he came in as a freshman. Yeah, he came in [as a freshman] and looked like a big kid, but by the time he was a sophomore he had filled out. He had put on like fifteen pounds."

• • •

Whoever lost the competition for the starting job between Wilcox and Holden would be the first post player off the bench. The first perimeter player would be Nicholas, the 6-3 Long Island native who had worked hard to distance himself from his reputation as just an outside shooter.

At one time, Nicholas had done little to discourage this reputation. On his left breast was a tattoo that read "The Specialist." In 2001–02, though, Nicholas would be anything but a specialist. The junior was going to be the backup point guard to Blake, the backup shooting guard to Dixon, and the backup small forward to Mouton. Nicholas knew he wasn't going to beat out any of those players for a starting spot, but he also was aware that he could earn plenty of minutes by playing each position.

The team's other returning players—Earl Badu, Matt Slaninka, and Calvin McCall—probably would not play much.

Badu, a senior walk-on point guard, had become a fan favorite; if he played, it meant the game was well out of reach. He also was one of Juan Dixon's closest friends. Both were from Baltimore, and they would often spend much of the night in their apartment discussing upcoming opponents and strategies.

Slaninka, meanwhile, was the tallest player in school history at 7-4. But the DeMatha High product, who had redshirted the previous season, could not get up and down the court, and it became obvious that he was a project. In fact, even before the season started, Slaninka would decide to transfer to tiny Shepherd College in West Virginia, and his departure wouldn't even be a blip on the radar screen.

Then there was McCall, a junior who had been the starting quarterback on the school's football team but had dropped that sport to pursue basketball.

"I felt more comfortable with [basketball], more excited about it," McCall said. "I would go to football practice and even games, and I wasn't really excited. I know a lot of people might look at it and say, 'What's this guy thinking?' To me, it was a personal decision. I'm not doing this out here for anybody else. I wanted to do what is best for me. I had to go to practice. I had to go to games. And this is what I felt more comfortable doing. I love coming to the gym every day to play ball. I can't say I loved playing football every day.

"One thing about football: If you're not into it fully, especially at the quarterback position, you're going to get yourself hurt, and I didn't want to do that."

Despite his obvious enthusiasm for basketball, McCall lacked the quickness to be a guard and the size to play forward, so his playing time would be limited.

That left it pretty much up to the team's three new members to provide some much-needed depth. In the past, Williams at times had gone with a seven-player rotation, but he preferred getting an eighth player in the mix to avoid tiring out the regulars before the season was over.

Naturally, none of the newcomers—junior college transfer Ryan Randle, prep-schooler Andre Collins, and Mike Grinnon—arrived with much fanfare. Randle had been somewhat disappointing in his sophomore year at Allegany Community College in Cumberland, Maryland; Collins, listed at a mere 5-9, would have to play point guard, where the Terrapins already had Blake and Nicholas; Grinnon had been bound for Princeton to play in the Tigers' back-door offense until Maryland decided to offer a scholarship.

On paper, the group hardly was overwhelming. To the critics, the three were just more recruits who only *ate* at McDonald's, particularly Grinnon, whose best statistics were in the classroom. He brought with him an 1160 on the SAT—"without studying"—and a cumulative 94 average in high school.

"Going to Princeton, it obviously was not the level of Maryland [in basketball], but it had so much more to offer in fields of life," Grinnon said. "A lot of people don't get to go to Princeton. But Maryland, in a basketball aspect, gave me an opportunity to prove myself.

"That's what I think is really interesting about the whole thing. Gary Williams is not afraid to give people a shot who are no-names coming out of high school. Look at Juan and Lonny. That's them to a tee. He does what he thinks will help the program and I trust him."

As soon as Maryland offered a scholarship, Grinnon accepted. A few other ACC schools then made inquiries, as did Notre Dame and Boston College. Grinnon, though, was sold on Maryland, where a former high school opponent, Nicholas, was enjoying success. Still, to play in the ACC, he would need to make a big adjustment, as he learned the moment he began playing with his new teammates during the summer before school started.

"Basketball-wise, obviously the talent from the high school I was at, the level I was used to, was a huge jump," Grinnon said. "The intensity was the main thing, how hard everybody plays all the time. In high school, if you are better than other people you can take breaks and pace yourself.

"The first time I played [with the Maryland team], I remember Wilcox got it in the post. I came over to help, and he put one of the meanest dunks I've ever seen right on my head. It took me about two weeks until I felt comfortable."

Like Grinnon, Collins felt as if he had achieved something big just by getting to College Park. He had grown up in Crisfield, Maryland, a town of three thousand on the Eastern Shore where the main industry is picking the meat out of the Chesapeake Bay's blue crabs. Just making it out of town can be challenging for a teenager.

"Most of my friends now are either locked up or selling drugs or something like that," Collins said. "I've been there all my life. I wouldn't say it's a bad town, but it's not somewhere where many dreams come true, where many people [try to] excel, to do good things."

Getting out was difficult for Collins, who failed to score high enough on the SAT to be eligible to play as a freshman. He spent a postgraduate year at Hargrave Military Academy in Chatham, Virginia, about twenty-five miles north of the North Carolina state line—the same school that Baxter had attended to qualify academically.

Randle, too, had academic problems coming out of high school. While most of the nation's top athletes take the SAT over and over and over to try to reach a qualifying score, Randle, a student at Duncanville High in the Dallas suburbs, never even took the test, because he had always believed he was headed to a junior college. He never really worried about the SAT, he said, because "nobody really recruited me my junior or senior year." So, following the suggestion of University of Texas coach Rick Barnes, he enrolled at Maryland's Allegany Community College. Barnes was familiar with Allegany from his previous job, at Clemson, where he had lost a fierce recruiting battle for guard Steve Francis.

It was at Allegany that Randle earned his high school diploma; he said that at Duncanville he had been unable to pass the math portion of the exit exam required by the State of Texas in order to graduate from high school.

At Allegany, Randle enjoyed a good freshman season, averaging 10.2 points and 5.1 rebounds. When the early signing period rolled around in November 2000, Randle accepted a scholarship from Maryland.

His future plans solidified, Randle failed to meet expectations as a sophomore. His averages went up to 13.2 points and 7.8 rebounds per game, but more was anticipated from a big man who had a scholarship waiting from a top ACC program. Some Maryland fans, after seeing Randle play, wondered why he had merited a scholarship.

Playing time was available—after all, someone had to take the 10.2 minutes per game played the previous season by Mike Mardesich. And having one more large body off the bench to complement Baxter, Holden, and Wilcox could give Williams a very deep rotation.

But Randle, it appeared, was not in great shape, particularly when compared with Baxter, who spent countless extra hours in the weight room and running on the court.

From just one look, it was apparent that until his arrival in College Park, Randle had had to use a map to find the weight room. He was a little pudgy and needed to learn how to eat healthier. If anything, he was a McDonald's All-American at the dining table. Add into the mix the hangdog, droopy-eyed look Randle always sported—one that quickly earned him the nickname "Sleepy"—and it was easy to think that Randle was not always going as hard as he needed to.

"When he first came in, he didn't understand what it took to really be in shape to play the game, and strengthwise he didn't know it either," said Kurtis Shultz, a former Maryland player who was now the team's strength-and-conditioning coach.

It did not take long for Randle to find out.

• • •

The team started its fall workouts during the second week of school, giving everyone a week to adjust to classes. The first workout was scheduled for September 10, a Monday, and the first group—the three newcomers, receiving bottom-of-the-totem-pole treatment—was due in at 6:45 A.M., a time when college dorms are silent while students sleep away the previous night's fun.

By 7:30, Randle was running to the locker room. He was so out of shape that the workout had caused him to vomit.

"That was tough," Randle said. "I never wake up at 6:45. It was my first time. I didn't know what to expect. I went to bed early, too. Once we stopped, my body couldn't go anymore.

"It seemed like it took forever [to get to the bathroom]. Everything was moving in slow motion. Once I got in there, then everything was moving too fast."

It took only a few minutes for word to spread.

"First day. First lift. I had to tell everybody," Shultz recalled with a wide grin.

It was a story that would be retold throughout the season. But a few team members offered some counseling.

"I was thinking I was out of shape and everything wasn't right until Drew told me he almost did it, too, when he was a freshman," Randle said. "That made me feel good about it."

Said Grinnon, who was up by 6 A.M. that day so that he could eat well before working out, "That definitely showed him how tough things were. I was actually relieved. It made me feel better because I know I definitely was dying. Seeing him struggle, too, made me feel better."

During preseason workouts in September, Shultz put in extra sessions with Randle, running sprints with the player in an attempt to motivate him. He also put Randle through boxing and kickboxing workouts to keep the player's heart rate higher for longer periods of time. Running around the basketball court, Randle could occasionally catch a breather; sparring with Shultz offered no such respites.

"He couldn't even put twenty-five-pound dumbbells over his head for ten reps," Shultz said of Randle. "He was pretty weak. He just had never lifted before. The good thing about Ryan is he works really hard and was really receptive. He never once has been a problem. Ever. He would come in almost every Saturday and lift on the optional day."

Shultz has the physique of a football player and the menacing look of a bar bouncer, light reflecting off his shaved head. At DeMatha High School in Hyattsville, just down the road from College Park, he played basketball for coaching legend Morgan Wootten. Then he joined the Maryland team in 1992, appearing in sixty-seven games in his college career. While his role was limited, Shultz played a key part in one of the most important victories during Williams's tenure, an 84–83 overtime victory over Georgetown in the 1993–94 season opener, the first meeting between the teams in more than thirteen years. Usually, though, Shultz had a good view from the bench.

"I loved to lift," Shultz said. "I loved the conditioning part. I always loved the running and conditioning. It's always been in my blood. When I grew up, I was a little fat kid—I was always trying to condition."

When asked about the relatively scant highlights from his playing days, Shultz laughed. "Luckily, we have two pictures in the locker room from the two Sweet Sixteen teams and I'm in there. There's me when I had hair."

After graduating, Shultz opened his own business and became one of the most successful personal trainers in the region. His clients include several Baltimore Ravens, including All-Pro linebacker Ray Lewis.

In the fall of 2001, Shultz was entering his third season at Maryland, and there was little question that he had played a significant role in the program's emergence. Each year, Maryland's team, as a whole, was one of the strongest teams in the nation, something it had not always been.

The 1998–99 season—Juan Dixon's freshman year, and better known around College Park as the "Steve Francis Season"—was a record-setting one for Maryland, but it ended in disappointment. The Terrapins established new school marks for total victories (twenty-eight) and ACC victories (thirteen) in a season and earned a number-two seed in the NCAA tournament for just the second time ever, but they were left with a sour feeling after losing to St. John's, 76–62, in the Sweet Sixteen.

To many fans, it was just another case of Maryland's failing to win when it mattered most. The Terrapins, with their flashy superstar, had breezed through much of the regular season; twenty-four of the team's twenty-eight victories were by more than ten points.

But against St. John's, Maryland had been pushed around, looking like many of the teams the Terrapins had brushed aside throughout the season. It was a problem that had to be fixed, and within a few days, assistant coach Jimmy Patsos called Kurtis Shultz to see if he was interested in helping his old team bulk up. Shultz agreed to work with the team that spring, and during those workouts in the football weight room, Shultz found an ally in the skinny freshman Dixon.

Shultz had met Dixon in 1998 when they were playing against each other in a pickup game at the Jewish Community Center in Owings

Mills, outside of Baltimore. Forget that Shultz and Dixon were graduates of Catholic high schools and now found themselves going at it at the JCC. What is more interesting is the thought of the hulking Shultz matched up against the spindly Dixon.

"I'm just knocking this kid around and I'm thinking, 'This kid is going to Maryland?'" Shultz said. "I wasn't the best player in the world."

But, Shultz remembered, once they got in the weight room at Maryland, Dixon gave him "the biggest respect of anybody. He was always very receptive."

And over the next few years, Dixon developed a great deal of strength. "Juan Dixon, when I first got here, couldn't bench-press 135 pounds," Shultz said. "By the end of [his] last year, he could do 185 for ten reps. That's a lot for a guy his size." Dixon's upper body and arms, by his senior year, were so muscular that it looked as though one could insert a pin to deflate him.

Shultz's other top project was Lonny Baxter. At first, Baxter was hesitant to believe in Shultz's weight program, agility drills, and running. Like most players coming out of high school, he had dominated on sheer ability, and he had been so much bigger and taller than most of the players around him that he hadn't needed to lift weights. Eventually, though, Baxter bought into Shultz's regimen, and within two years he had shed pounds of baby fat and added muscle mass to his upper body. The transformation was remarkable. Baxter did extra running and changed his diet, scrapping red meats in favor of fish and chicken.

"Lonny said, 'I need to get in shape,'" Shultz recalled. "That's all he had to say. The good thing about Lonny was that he worked hard in the weight room."

So in 2001, with team leaders Dixon and Baxter backing the program, Shultz found that Maryland's players embraced his training sessions.

"The first time I met with the guys, I told them, 'I'm not in the babysitting business. That's not my job. If you're grown men, you're going to work hard,'" Shultz said. "I think me telling them that and treating them like men, I think that's a better way to go about it. It's a better way to go about it than treating them like little kids."

Dixon, in particular, was a great motivator for the team. "A college kid is going to have his days. Some days you've got a lot of studying to do and you're not going to want to lift," Shultz said. "But the thing I liked about Juan was that he always brought energy to the weight room. He would get on Lonny—'Get in shape, fat boy.' It was always fun.

"I told the players, they need to come to the weight room and [to] their [agility training sessions] with their attitude. Juan and I had yelling matches. That's fine. If you've got a problem, come see me. I'm not going to be an ass in the weight room. I want that energy in there.

"You need somebody who will be competitive and won't take any shit. And that's Juan."

With motivated players pushing themselves, and also established stars and team leaders like Dixon and Baxter pushing their teammates even harder, Maryland's summer workouts prior to the 2001–02 season were particularly effective. Summer workouts are supposed to be voluntary, because the NCAA doesn't want the players to be forced into any activity. But at most of the nation's top programs, attendance for summer workouts is better than the average class attendance for the general student body. In some places, the message comes down from coaches that the players had better get in the weight room during June, July, and August. At other schools, like Maryland, the players put the pressure on themselves to make it to the "voluntary" sessions; some know that if they want playing time, they need to get in better shape, while others exert peer pressure on their teammates in an effort to maximize the team's potential.

In the summer, Maryland's voluntary workouts consisted of weight lifting and agility drills three days a week and running once a week. So when the team began its fall conditioning that Monday morning in early

September, many of the players—or at least the veterans—were already in good shape. Newcomers like Ryan Randle had more work to do.

During the Monday-morning workouts, after Shultz trained the first-year players at 6:45, he moved to the veterans. The 7:45 group included Holden, Baxter, Wilcox, and Mouton. It was a group Shultz dreaded because of the fierceness with which each member competed during the King of the Lane drill, in which a player goes one-on-one with Shultz, trying to use his gluteus maximus to push the strength coach out of the lane.

"That was the worst," Shultz said. "I thought I was going to be smart one day and leave Byron for last, but he was the best, he had all the leverage. Must have been from wrestling all those alligators. It's almost Greco-Roman wrestling, [but] we don't throw each other to the ground. I do if they piss me off."

Then there were lifting sessions on Tuesday and Thursday afternoons and running on Thursday nights. When he left on Thursday, Shultz always tacked up a lifting schedule in the weight room for anyone who wanted to get in an optional lift on Saturday.

Chris Wilcox was one of the few players who had taken to weight lifting before getting to Maryland. And it showed. Even as a freshman, Wilcox stood out because of his muscles, a rarity for a basketball player just a few months removed from high school. In the small town of Whiteville, North Carolina, he had had plenty of free time on his hands, and he had picked up weight lifting from his best friend, Carlos Geathers, an avid lifter.

And now, entering his sophomore year, Wilcox was creating problems for Maryland in the weight room—though they were good problems.

"He was the one we had to order more weights for," Shultz said. "We didn't have enough dumbbells. They only went up to seventy pounds. We ordered up to a hundred pounds because he was so strong."

• • •

The preseason workouts took on special importance this season, because Maryland would play the earliest season opener in school history, November 8 against Arizona in the Coaches vs. Cancer Classic in Madison Square Garden. Not only was there less time for players to work themselves into shape once practice started, but those first few weeks of practice were going to be particularly rigorous, with precious little time to waste.

"The first four weeks, practice had to be really intense," Shultz said. "Coach was saying we had to step up the conditioning, we had to go into practice in condition. It helped that we were a veteran team."

Gary Williams was leaning on his strength coach and his players, with good reason. He knew all the pieces were in place and the 2001–02 season had the potential to be special. Maryland, Williams believed, was one of the top teams in the nation, and as he soon would announce, his goal was nothing less than the national championship. Williams had followed a long and difficult path to get to this point, and he wanted to make the most of this opportunity.

CHAPTER 3

Gary

Gary Williams was similar to most of the other young boys growing up in Collingswood, New Jersey, in the 1950s. He liked to play sports—football in the fall, basketball in the winter, and baseball in the spring.

"It was easy to just grow up in sports," he said. "Nobody had any money, so it was a very cheap way to grow up. You don't need money to play sports. Nobody had a car back then. You basically walked where you wanted to go."

He was the second of three boys born to Shirley and William Williams: Douglas was sixteen months older than Gary, David seven years younger. But Gary was close to neither of his siblings. Perhaps the age difference prevented a relationship with David. And while Gary was always chasing a ball around some athletic field, Douglas spent much of his time around cars.

"That's the way it was, either sports or cars back then," Gary said. "So that was okay."

Life in the Williams household was mundane. Shirley, whose given name was Helen, worked as a receptionist for a nearby car dealer. William

Williams processed checks for the Federal Reserve Bank in Philadelphia—in the days before computers and sophisticated machinery, somebody had to sort which checks had to be sent to which banks.

The Williamses weren't a particularly close family, but they were religious. William and Shirley taught Sunday school until they retired, and William was a deacon in the Presbyterian Church. The boys became accustomed to spending several hours a week in church.

"That was a big part of growing up, going to church," Gary said. "You didn't have a choice in the matter. You went."

Gary did have a choice when it came to sports. And the choice he made was to play as much as he could. As a youngster, Williams spent countless hours across Taylor Avenue at Sharp Elementary School or down the street at Knights Park competing in some athletic endeavor. He was the quarterback in football, played point guard in basketball, and either pitched or played the outfield when it came to baseball, though it soon became clear which sport was his love.

Williams quarterbacked the football team at Collingswood Junior High School but gave up the sport before high school. He continued to play baseball, though he thinks his affinity for basketball got in the way of his ability to excel on the diamond. While he had a decent arm and was a good athlete, Williams never could master the fine art of hitting a curveball and struggled at the plate.

"For baseball, I was a good size. I was pretty big for baseball," Williams said. "I could run, I could throw okay. But I never put the time into it. By the time I got to junior high, in the summertime I was playing basketball all the time. I would play the high school season, that was only about twenty games."

It was on the basketball court that Williams was at his best. He wasn't much of a scorer, but he had a knack for passing the ball and playing good defense, two traits that can be tough to find in younger players. While he was quiet and said little off the court, on the court he was a leader.

"I was pretty shy," he said. But he admitted that his persona changed as soon as he laced a pair of cleats or high-tops. "Sports were always where you could let it out. I really thought I had a different personality on the court or baseball field than I did just being around. I didn't date much in high school. I just played. I was very confident in sports. I wasn't that confident, I guess, in a lot of other areas."

On the court, on the field, on the diamond, Gary could let it all hang out and show just how much he cared. Away from athletics, though, he often kept his feelings inside. That trend only intensified when Gary was thirteen and William and Shirley Williams separated.

Gary had been aware that his parents weren't getting along. He had overheard some of their disagreements and could sense the discord and tension. But their separation and subsequent divorce stunned him; divorce was something that just didn't happen in Collingswood. Gary can still remember the morning that his father abruptly delivered the news as he drove Gary to school: Mr. Williams would not be coming home that night.

Almost instantly, Gary felt like an outcast. In class or among friends, he felt "almost embarrassed" at what was happening between his parents, a feeling he never shared at the time with his ball-playing friends. Instead, he spent as much time as possible in the comfort of athletics, even though he received little encouragement from either of his parents to pursue such activity.

"I was good at sports, and I probably jumped into it even more because everything is equal on the court," Williams said. "Nobody counts how many parents you have or whether your parents are divorced."

He found refuge in local parks and at school, often playing one-on-one with Collingswood freshman basketball coach Neil Thompson. There were many nights when Williams would not get home until 8:30.

Growing up across the Delaware River from Philadelphia, Williams yearned to play in the Big Five, the group of schools that played their games at the city's famous Palestra: La Salle, Pennsylvania, Villanova, Temple, and St. Joseph's. Williams particularly liked the way St. Joseph's played. Coached by future Hall of Famer Jack Ramsay, the Hawks had little guards who played fast, something that particularly appealed to the 5-foot-10-inch Williams. As he moved through high school, Williams also was interested in Penn, where he hoped to join his high school buddy Stan Pawlak.

But Williams's report cards—full of B's and C's—weren't quite enough to cut it in the Ivy League. He made unofficial trips to look at St. Joseph's and visited Clemson, Pittsburgh, and Providence. It was in College Park, however, where Williams found himself a new home, smitten with the size and feel of Cole Field House.

Built at a cost of $3.3 million, the arena bore the name "The Student Activities Building" when it opened in December 1955. A year later, it was named after Judge William P. Cole, the alumnus who had chaired the university's Board of Regents for several years. It was one of the nation's largest arenas—in fact, some thought it too big. To Williams, it felt like the right fit.

Williams's playing career was rather unremarkable, perhaps his best season gaining the least amount of attention.

At the time, the NCAA prohibited freshmen from playing varsity sports, so each school fielded a freshman team. And in Williams's first year at Maryland, he helped that team to a 16–1 record.

He became a starter on the varsity the following year, and the team finished 18–8 overall and 10–4 in the ACC before losing to North Carolina State, 76–67, in the semifinals of the conference tournament, played at State's Reynolds Coliseum. Since back in those days only the ACC champion qualified for the NCAA tournament, Maryland's season was over despite its stellar record.

That was pretty much it for the highlights. The following season, with many returning players and the addition of a talented sophomore class,

Maryland fizzled, going 14–11. It was a difficult season for Williams, who midway through the schedule lost his starting job. And Coach Bud Millikan, like most coaches of the time, used his reserves only if a starter was extremely tired or in foul trouble, leaving Williams scant playing time. Although Williams was not happy, there was little he could do.

"It was all yes-sir or no-sir back then," Williams remembered. "There was no dialogue between player and coach. You were very respectful of your coach."

Williams moved back into the starting lineup and was a team captain as a senior. He made his way into the school's record book by making all eight of his field goal attempts in a 65–63 loss to South Carolina, to that point the most shots without a miss by a Maryland player. But that was one of only a few bright spots in a season in which the Terrapins finished 11–14, losing their final six games and prompting a coaching change.

Having completed his eligibility, Williams went off to northeastern Pennsylvania to attend a tryout for the Wilkes-Barre Barons of the old Eastern League. But it didn't take long for him to be cut, so soon he was in Fort Wayne, Indiana, to attend an insurance-sales training school run by the Lincoln National Life Insurance Company. That, too, proved futile, because it took almost no time for Williams to realize that going door-to-door making cold calls did not sound like much fun.

So needing a few more credits to earn his degree in business, he returned to College Park in the fall of 1967. If he wanted to stay involved in organized basketball, Williams had two choices. He could get into coaching, or (and some people no doubt will find this funny) he could try his hand at officiating.

In exchange for tuition and books, Williams opted to work as an assistant coach for Maryland's freshman team, at the time coached by Tom Davis. (He also officiated a few intramural games for five bucks a pop.)

While Williams did not know it at the time, that school year would be one of the most important in his life. He got his first coaching job, and in

February, during a break in the season, he returned home for a weekend and married his high school sweetheart, Diane. They had begun dating during Gary's senior year at Collingswood (Diane was a year younger), and they remained together even as he went to Maryland and Diane eventually went to nursing school in Camden. They were married in a church in Collingswood, then took a fiscally responsible, three-day honeymoon to Washington, D.C., before settling into an apartment off University Boulevard, less than one mile from campus.

With his personal life starting to take shape, Williams began to create his personality as a coach. Just as he was when he still wore a uniform, Williams was fiery, rarely holding back—though few noticed, because who would be paying attention to the assistant coach for a freshman team?

"It's funny. From the day I started coaching I was that way," Williams said. "I went from being a player, and playing you can really play hard. If you coach hard, then it looks like you're jumping up and down."

• • •

With the Vietnam War dominating the headlines, Gary Williams graduated from Maryland in the spring of 1968 and soon had his first full-time job, as the junior varsity basketball coach at Woodrow Wilson High School in Camden, New Jersey, close to his home in Collingswood. His friend Stan Pawlak's father was a teacher at the school, and when a vacancy arose, the elder Pawlak had passed Williams's name along to the head coach, Art DiPatri.

"I was very fortunate," Williams said. "I got a teaching deferment because it was an underprivileged area. Otherwise I would have been drafted."

Several times in the years to come, Williams would think to himself, "What if I had been drafted?" One of his close friends was drafted, went to Vietnam, and was killed at age twenty-two. Other friends were more fortunate and came back alive.

"I didn't have a plan coming out of college," Williams said. "That was my only offer I had to teach and coach. I didn't really put out résumés or anything like that. I got lucky, because I'm sure I would have gone in the draft if I didn't get that job. That's just the way it worked."

Diane got a job as a nurse, and Gary, along with his coaching duties, taught retailing, consumer education, and business law—all classes designated for students unlikely to attend college. It was an experience that Williams thinks helped his personal growth, dealing with many youngsters from tough backgrounds who had few adult figures in their lives. Life on the court came with some perks, too: Williams got to wash uniforms, occasionally drive the team bus to away games, and make sure his players got something to eat before each game.

"You had to do everything back then," he said, adding that there were many a pregame trip to the cheesesteak shop across the street from school.

"That's when I found out you could have discipline and be a tough guy at practice and still have them feel close to you. They have to believe you have them in your best interests."

Additionally, Williams said he had to adjust his style because societal norms were changing rapidly.

"There was a big change socially from 1968 to 1972," he said, pointing out the differences at the University of Maryland. "When I left, women still had visiting hours during the week. By ten o'clock, they had to be in their own dormitory. Four years later, there were coed dorms. Everything hit—the war, protesting, the riots. We didn't have school for two weeks in 1970 because kids were fighting. It was race. It was always fights over girls and things like that, a black guy dated a white girl. That was a tough change for a lot of people there."

Williams thought that basketball gave him an advantage when it came to dealing with race issues. He had played at Maryland when Billy Jones became the ACC's first black player. And when Williams played at

Collingswood, the Panthers had an all-white team, but he was exposed to black players from Camden, Trenton, and other places.

"Everybody just played ball," he said. "You grew up in a situation where a lot of adults didn't feel that way. They felt different people were different. It was Irish even against Italians. People were funny back then. And then the color thing, there was no socializing at all. People don't like change. Like my father—with him, the government was always right, there was no debate. And when kids started to wear their hair long, it meant they were on drugs. It was very rigid. There was no debate with adults back then. This was the way it was and you accepted it."

After one season of coaching Woodrow Wilson's junior varsity team, Williams got a promotion after Art DiPatri took another coaching job. In his first season as a head coach, Williams guided his team to a 27–0 record, including a victory over powerhouse East Orange High in the state championship game at the Atlantic City Convention Hall. Soon after, on April 11, Diane delivered the couple's first child, a daughter named Kristin.

At age twenty-five, Gary Williams had completed his playing career, moved back to New Jersey, been promoted to a head coach, won a state title, and become a father. It was a whirlwind.

If only he knew what lay ahead.

• • •

Already a husband and a father, Gary Williams was beginning to look into the future. He had just finished his second season as the head coach at Woodrow Wilson High School and he liked his job, as a coach and as a teacher, and envisioned himself making a career out of it.

Gary and Diane had used a small inheritance as a down payment for their first house, a two-story, three-bedroom house with a nice backyard in nearby Haddon Heights. In short, life was good.

Then the phone rang. It was Tom Davis, under whom Williams had been an assistant coach for Maryland's freshman team. Davis had left Maryland to become the head coach at Lafayette College, a small Division I school in Easton, Pennsylvania. Now he had the opportunity to hire the school's first full-time assistant basketball coach and wanted to hire Williams. Naturally, there was a catch. The assistant basketball coach also had to be the school's head soccer coach.

"I turned it down," Williams said. "I was afraid. I felt comfortable [at Woodrow Wilson]. It was where I grew up. I thought we could have a good team that next year. Plus, I don't know anything about soccer. It's the old story, you never want to do anything you're not comfortable with. A player always practices what he is good at; it's hard to get him to practice something he is not good at. It was the same thing for me. I had a comfort zone."

Davis, though, would not take no for an answer. He asked how many other college coaches Williams knew, and how many might hire Williams if they had an opportunity. This, Davis implored, was the one and only chance the high school coach would ever have to get into the collegiate ranks. Williams wasn't a go-getter. While the eager beavers of coaching spent their summers in the Poconos working the Five-Star camp and networking, Williams worked as director of the neighborhood youth corps in Camden to make a few extra bucks.

Davis told Williams that if he didn't like college coaching, he could always go back to high schools, but that if he stayed in high schools, he couldn't always go to a college job. The message got through. Soon Gary and Diane packed up, rented out their house, and moved with Kristin to Easton, a city of fifty thousand about eighty miles north of Philadelphia on the Delaware River.

In addition to coaching on another level, Williams had to learn how to coach another sport. He had never played soccer, and if he had a choice, he wouldn't be coaching it. But Williams *was* coaching soccer, and he knew he could not fake his lack of experience.

"Look, here's the deal," Williams remembered telling the players during his first meeting with them. "I'm not a soccer guy. But I know sports. I think I know what it takes to win. But with the drills, you have to demonstrate."

The drills, Williams learned, were similar to what he would put his team through on a basketball court, with one exception: instead of their hands, the players used their feet. As he grew more comfortable, Williams started to participate in practice.

"I played goalie," he said. "It was fun. I was in my twenties. I liked it."

And he could use his hands.

Somehow, with a coach who knew little about the sport, Lafayette's soccer team finished 6–5–2 that season, a record that Williams remains proud of. The soccer team went winless in 1973, but rebounded to set what was then the school record for victories in a season by going 9–2–2 in 1974.

"You're a long way away from the action in soccer," Williams said. "In basketball you're a lot closer. Plus, not many people came to our games. And officiating back then in soccer was not what it is today. You had a lot of officials who didn't play soccer much either. It was an interesting combination, a coach who didn't play and officials who didn't play. But you look back and that was very valuable for me. You learned to appreciate guys—those soccer guys worked as hard as the basketball guys. You respect that."

Coaching soccer provided Williams the chance to be a collegiate head coach. And while it was not in his sport of choice, he had to deal with several concerns that basketball coaches face every day. He learned how to handle players, how to deal with issues of playing time, and how best to use a budget. Perhaps the most bothersome thing for Williams was that during the latter part of the soccer season, he would miss most of basketball practice because he had to be loyal to his soccer players.

"It was frustrating," Williams said. "But at the same time you didn't want to screw the kids who were playing."

On the basketball court, Davis and Williams proved a formidable tandem. Lafayette went 21–6 that first season, starting a run of six consecutive winning seasons for the Leopards. By his sixth season at Lafayette, in 1976, Williams had settled in. He and Diane sold their house in New Jersey and bought a place in Easton off Twenty-fifth Street, a few miles from Lafayette. It would be their first of many real estate transactions in the next few years.

With Davis guiding Lafayette to three twenty-win seasons and a 116–44 record in six years, it was only a matter of time before he moved up the coaching food chain. The offer came from Boston College, and when Davis accepted it, Williams had a choice to make. He could remain at Lafayette as the head basketball coach or go to Boston as Davis's assistant.

"I probably should have taken the head job, but Tom had been so successful, I wasn't sure if I could do that," Williams said. "And I hadn't recruited with scholarships"—because unlike most Division I schools, Lafayette did not offer athletic-based scholarships. "I thought that was important."

• • •

Williams had never been to Boston before, and he didn't stay long in Beantown. One year later, after Jim Lynam left American University to return to his alma mater, St. Joseph's, Williams had another chance to become a head basketball coach. Davis and Rutgers coach Tom Young called American University athletic director Bob Frailey to put in a good word for Williams. Soon the deal was done, and it was time to call the realtor yet again.

American U. presented challenges like few other schools. The home gym was at Fort Myer in Arlington, Virginia, which was not that far away but seemed a world apart from American's campus in upper northwest Washington. The Eagles went 14–13 and 13–14 in Williams's first two seasons, as the coach struggled to balance his enthusiasm against the fear of doing something completely new.

"I was excited and scared," Williams said. "I realized I wasn't as prepared as I thought I was." Finally, in his third season, in 1980–81, Williams guided American to a school-record 24–6, including an 11–0 mark in the East Coast Conference and a berth in the National Invitation Tournament (NIT). It was then, he said, that he knew he was a good coach.

"I always thought that I could coach, I always thought I knew the game," he said. "I always studied the game. Like when I played, I knew the game pretty well. It was just something I liked. I didn't like a lot of things, but I liked basketball. I enjoyed the mental part of it."

After a 21–9 season and another NIT berth in the 1981–82 season, it was again time for Gary, Diane, and Kristin to pack up. Tom Davis had left Boston College for Stanford, and BC turned to Davis's former assistant as his replacement.

It would be a mammoth leap for Williams. After coaching in the East Coast Conference, which didn't even have an automatic NCAA tournament bid for its champion, he suddenly found himself coaching in the powerful Big East Conference, surrounded by some of the game's best-known and most-respected coaches. There was John Thompson at Georgetown, Jim Boeheim at Syracuse, Rollie Massimino at Villanova, and Lou Carnesecca at St. John's. Did Williams belong among this select group?

"I never looked down at the other bench in terms of who you're coaching against," Williams said.

Back in Boston, Williams did what he had done throughout his coaching career: he won. While Georgetown had Patrick Ewing and St. John's had Chris Mullin, Boston College did not have overwhelming talent, but it did have an incredibly intense coach and gritty players. In his first season in Chestnut Hill, 1982–83, Williams guided the Eagles to a

25–7 record, a share of the Big East Conference regular season title, and a berth in the NCAA tournament.

It was the first time Williams experienced college basketball's main event, and, in what would become a trend, his team was sent far from home, this time out to Corvallis, Oregon. Seeded fourth in the West Region, BC received a first-round bye, then beat twelfth-seeded Princeton, 51–42, to advance to the Sweet Sixteen. Moving on to Ogden, Utah, the Eagles lost to top-seeded Virginia, 95–92.

Boston College lost in the second round of the NIT in 1984, then advanced to the NCAA tournament Sweet Sixteen again in 1985. Seeded eleventh, the Eagles went to Houston and upset sixth-seeded Texas Tech, 55–53. In the second round, BC faced third-seeded Duke, which was coming off its first NCAA tournament victory under thirty-eight-year-old coach Mike Krzyzewski and was now the nation's tenth-ranked team. Led by diminutive guard Michael Adams, though, BC pulled the upset, 74–73; it was perhaps the first landmark victory in Williams's coaching career and added to the general consensus that he was a coach on the rise.

A year later, despite a 13–15 record, Williams was out of Boston, accepting an offer to become head coach at Ohio State.

• • •

As Gary Williams took over an Ohio State team that was coming off an NIT championship, his alma mater was in disarray.

Under Lefty Driesell, Maryland had become a solid team, never finishing with a losing record in the Left-hander's seventeen seasons. In the 1980s, Driesell's teams had won fewer than nineteen games just once and had played in the NCAA tournament in six of seven seasons.

The Terrapins weren't quite the "UCLA of the East" that Driesell had promised, but they were more than respectable. And with a 6-8 forward named Len Bias, they were just plain exciting.

Bias was one of the sport's most dazzling players, with a graceful jump shot and the athleticism to slam-dunk the ball so hard that it left a lasting memory. As a sophomore, he was named the most valuable player of the Atlantic Coast Conference tournament, leading Maryland to its first tournament championship. As a junior and again as a senior, Bias was named an All-American and the Atlantic Coast Conference player of the year, the only Terrapin ever to win that award twice. Maryland was 88–44 with Bias on the roster, and Lenny left College Park as the all-time leading scorer in school history, with 2,149 points.

On June 17, 1986, Bias was the second overall pick in the NBA's annual college draft, going to the league-champion Boston Celtics, who had acquired the pick in a trade with the Seattle SuperSonics. Standing on a stage in New York's Madison Square Garden, Bias posed for pictures with league commissioner David Stern. Bias then agreed to an endorsement contract with the shoe company Reebok for a reported $325,000. Combined with the annual salary he was to receive from the Celtics, Bias was going to be a millionaire, which in those days was quite a feat for a rookie ballplayer.

But in the wee hours of the morning on June 19, in his suite in Maryland's Washington Hall dormitory, Len Bias died of a cocaine overdose. He was twenty-two.

"It's the cruelest thing I've ever heard," Larry Bird, the Celtics' superstar, said upon hearing the news.

The death of Len Bias had ramifications across the country. Drug use became a much more serious matter. Drug testing was more accepted.

While tests revealed that Bias had ingested five times what would be considered a normal recreational amount, more than eleven thousand people packed into Cole Field House—the stage where Bias so often had performed to their delight—to mourn his passing. Celtics president Red Auerbach told those in attendance that the city of Boston had not been so traumatized since the assassination of President John F. Kennedy in

1963. The Reverend Jesse Jackson compared Bias's death to those of Jesus Christ, Dr. Martin Luther King, Mozart, and Gandhi.

"Lenny was vulnerable because all of us are vulnerable," Jackson told the crowd. "He is being used by God to save a generation. Tonight, the children mourn. Let us hope they learn."

There was a criminal probe, and under intense scrutiny, Maryland also conducted an internal investigation of the events surrounding Bias's death. Athletic director Dick Dull was reassigned, and on October 29, 1986, Driesell was forced to resign as head coach.

"There needed to be some redirection of our overall athletic program, particularly in relation to basketball," university chancellor John B. Slaughter said at a news conference to announce that Driesell had been reassigned to a job as assistant athletic director. "There needed to be a greater commitment to the development of the young men playing in the program. It is my belief that at this time, in order to make those changes, we would require new leadership."

Speaking at a separate news conference, Driesell read a brief statement and declined to answer questions. "It is obvious that the administration wants to make a coaching change, and I do not want to coach if I am not wanted," he said.

• • •

Three years later, on October 11, 1989, Maryland was back in the hunt for a new coach. Bob Wade resigned amid allegations that he had broken several NCAA rules. The *Washington Post* reported that Wade had signed a negotiated settlement while at Washington's Sibley Memorial Hospital recovering from back surgery.

Wade, the first black men's basketball head coach in the ACC, had entered into a difficult situation. Hired only one day after the announcement of Driesell's resignation, he was resented by many Maryland fans. They wondered if the coach at Baltimore's Dunbar High School could make the jump to the highly competitive ACC and why their chancellor, Slaughter, had sought advice from Georgetown coach John Thompson, who was despised by most Maryland fans.

Wade's three seasons included few bright spots. The Terrapins went zero for the ACC in 1986–87, advanced to the second round of the NCAA tournament in 1988, then won just one game in ACC play in the 1988–89 season before upsetting North Carolina State in the ACC tournament.

The on-court results, combined with another NCAA investigation, made it seem that things had gone from bad to worse.

As Maryland went in search of a replacement, it set its sights on Gary Williams. Williams was an alumnus of the university, had excellent credentials, knew the area, and coached an exciting brand of basketball. And while he was not actively seeking another job, it was a good time for Williams to leave Columbus. Though he had won fifty-eight games in three seasons and had landed perhaps the best recruit of his coaching career, shooting guard Jimmy Jackson, there was turbulence in Williams's personal life. The previous summer, he and Diane had separated. Perhaps getting a change of scenery would provide a fresh start.

Williams knew when he accepted the job that Maryland remained under investigation by the NCAA. But given precedent and the fact that the university was cooperating with investigators, he had no reason to believe that any penalties would be significant. When it was announced that Maryland would lose scholarships and would not be permitted to play in games televised live, and therefore would be unable to participate in the season-ending ACC tournament, Williams was stunned. He thought he had shot the worst air ball of his life—which might be saying something, considering he was a 45 percent shooter (53.9 percent from the line) in college—in leaving Ohio State for a program that might be crippled for years to come.

Three years later, though, Williams and Maryland were ready to challenge all comers. Led by freshmen Joe Smith and Keith Booth, in the season opener the Terrapins beat area rival Georgetown in overtime, 84–83. Maryland returned to the NCAA tournament that season, but perhaps more important was the addition of Booth, the team's first recruit from Baltimore in many years. In many ways, Booth's success eased tensions in and around College Park after Bob Wade's disastrous tenure as Maryland's coach. Booth's presence eventually made it easier for Williams to recruit others from the Charm City, like Rodney Elliott and a skinny kid named Juan Dixon.

CHAPTER 4

Juan

Coach Gary Williams stood in the hallway outside his team's locker room in Sacramento's Arco Arena. Maryland had just cruised to an 82–68 victory over Utah State in the first round of the 1998 NCAA tournament, and Williams had one thing on his mind: preparing for the Terrapins' second-round game.

Having taken care of his media obligations, Williams, still in the suit he wore during the game, gave a few final instructions to his staff. He had decided to let the players hang around to watch the first half of the Illinois–South Alabama game—Maryland would play the winner two days later—but he made it absolutely clear that at halftime, all the players were to meet, get on the bus, and head back to the hotel to get back to work.

Williams directed Troy Wainwright, who served then as the team's administrative assistant, to keep an eye on one particular player who was most likely to need a search party to locate him in time to make the bus.

"Assign one of the managers to make sure Juan-Don isn't late," the coach said.

Juan-Don was Juan Dixon, the nineteen-year-old shooting guard from Baltimore who had joined the team in late December. Although he had taken a longer road than most to get to Maryland, Dixon remained somewhat immature. He was full of enthusiasm, and sometimes could not handle that pent-up energy.

On a veteran team that started two seniors and three juniors, Dixon was the little kid who didn't quite know how to act and what to do. He had been in college for only a few months and would not play in a game until the next season. The prevailing thought was not to waste a season of Dixon's eligibility but rather to let him adjust to college life without the pressures that came along with playing basketball. He could practice with the team this season, sit on the bench, and see what it was all about, then have four seasons of eligibility remaining.

Occasionally during those practices in Cole Field House, Dixon would glance up at the jerseys hanging from the rafters: among them, McMillen, Elmore, King, Williams, Bias. Caught in a daydream, Dixon would imagine what it would be like to see his name and number hoisted to the top of the grand old building.

"But I never thought I would get that shot," he said.

Of course, Juan Dixon never met a shot he didn't like.

• • •

Growing up in East Baltimore, Dixon sought refuge on the city's blacktop basketball courts. On the asphalt, he could try to be a normal adolescent, not someone who had been through a childhood so tough that it would make anyone cringe.

Dixon's parents, Juanita and Phil Jr., were drug addicts who contracted HIV from using infected needles. Juanita died during Juan's sophomore year at Calvert Hall College High School; Phil passed on thirteen months later.

Thirty years earlier, Gary Williams had gone to the basketball court to get away from his parents' marital problems. Now Juan Dixon followed a similar pattern to get away from his life at home.

The Dixons hadn't been neglectful parents; they had plenty of rules for their children to follow, such as folding their clothes, staying off the living room couch, and respecting and obeying their elders.

"We had rules back in the day," Dixon said, "when we actually lived together."

But the lure and power of heroin always seemed to get in the way.

There were many times when Juan crashed with friends, cousins, aunts and uncles, or grandparents to avoid some of the tumult in his parents' lives.

The list of people who influenced Juan was long. Friends. Relatives. Teammates. Coaches. But there was never any question who was at the front of the line.

Phil Dixon III, Juan's older brother, was tough as nails, with a jump shot to match. Growing up, Phil played all the sports. In football, he was a quarterback; in baseball, a pitcher. Guess what positions Juan wanted to play when he took up those sports? In basketball, Phil went on to become a Division III All-American guard at Shenandoah University in Winchester, Virginia, twice earning Dixie Conference player of the year honors and graduating in 1996 as the school's all-time leading scorer.

Around the time Phil graduated, his younger brother was attracting attention on the basketball court. Maryland assistant coach Billy Hahn had stumbled onto Dixon the previous winter when one night Hahn went to watch his son's team play and one of the opposing team's players lit it up. Dixon was reed thin, but his shooting stroke was so smooth that it piqued Hahn's interest.

Maryland kept tabs on Dixon. A few months later, Williams and assistant coach Dave Dickerson watched Dixon play when they went to the Nike Peach Jam in Augusta, Georgia, one of the many summer showcases for traveling teams.

Summer basketball is full of ball hogs and selfish play, with most players simply out for themselves, trying to make a name and stand out to the college recruiters. Flashy dribbling and attempts at highlight-style dunking are the norm. Final scores matter little. Few people, if any, remember or even care which team won any given tournament. All they want to know is which player did what and who he did it to.

A few years earlier, when Williams recruited Joe Smith out of Norfolk, Smith played on a summer team with Allen Iverson, the future Georgetown Hoya and Philadelphia 76er who was regarded as one of the biggest gunners of all time. "How many shots do you think Joe got?" Williams asked with a grin. "Look at Iverson now. You can imagine what he did then."

So as he watched Dixon in a hot and stuffy gym in Augusta, what caught Williams's attention wasn't the player's shooting ability or any other true basketball skill. Instead, the coach became convinced that he was looking at a player when he saw Dixon diving for loose balls and hustling for rebounds even though his team was losing by twenty points in the final minutes of a game. In an era when top players pick and choose where and when and how hard they want to play, Dixon was something of a throwback.

"He played hard all the time," Williams said, recalling a trait he has always cherished. "It's nice to recruit guys who you don't have to try to make them play hard.

"And I guess I kind of always liked him personally. He could always put the ball in the basket. That was never a problem. The obvious problem was whether he was big enough. But [I] coached Michael Adams and Jay Burson [at Ohio State], and Iverson is a second guard. So why can't Juan be big enough?

"A guy has to have a certain talent level, but once they have that, a big part of it is liking the way a guy plays. Juan Dixon, I knew it would be fun coaching him."

Maryland's coaching staff had been recruiting Dixon, Albert Mouring from the Eastern Shore, and Alvin Brown from Washington, D.C., with the intention of giving a scholarship to one of the three. Dixon's willingness to hustle in a meaningless situation had made the difference.

Now that he had a scholarship offer, though, Juan Dixon had to qualify academically. He graduated from Calvert Hall in 1997 but lacked the SAT score necessary to play as a freshman. So Dixon spent the fall working with Gladys Bragg, the mother of his girlfriend, Robyn, to improve his test scores. That brought on another problem: Dixon did so well on the test that his score was flagged by the Educational Testing Service (ETS), which administers the exam, because the improvement seemed unrealistic. Rumors are rampant that top players cheat off others or even have someone else take the test for them, so perhaps it was inevitable that Dixon's raised score would draw attention.

Miss Gladys, as Juan called her, wanted to pursue legal remedies to have the score reinstated, but Dixon said to just let him retake the test. When he again did well, the ETS accepted the score and Dixon was ready to go to Maryland. It would be nearly another year, though, before he got to take the court in a meaningful game.

• • •

"I was just out there doing my thing, acting like a kid. Just goofing around, not being terribly serious," Dixon said of his first year at Maryland. "I was so intrigued by everything that goes on at a Division I program and playing with guys I actually looked up to in high school."

The next year, Dixon had the chance to learn up close from another role model. Steve Francis was the most exciting player to don a Maryland uniform since Len Bias. Though he was only 6 foot 3, Francis could jump so high that anything seemed possible. He could shoot the three, slash to the basket—and man, could he finish strong. Francis, too, had had a difficult upbringing, raised by a single mother who died at the age of thirty-nine, when Steve was just eighteen. He had barely played at all in high school, and he went to two junior colleges before arriving at Maryland in time for the 1998–99 season.

With Francis, a potential NBA superstar, in the fold, Dixon's role as a backup was clear. Francis was sensational, keeping the folks at ESPN's *SportsCenter* busy cutting the highlights as the Terrapins started the season with ten consecutive wins, only one of which was close. Among the romps were a 113–46 season-opening thumping of Western Carolina and a 70–54 dismantling of tenth-ranked UCLA in the Puerto Rico Shootout.

"By the end of that week, Steve Francis was probably going to the NBA," Gary Williams recalled, noting that because the NBA was in the midst of a players' strike at the time, Maryland was receiving prominent billing on highlight shows.

For Dixon and fellow freshman Lonny Baxter, an undersized center from Silver Spring, Maryland, the blowouts had benefits, such as playing time. Dixon made four of seven three-point tries and scored fourteen points in the Western Carolina victory, one of twelve games in which he scored in double figures that season. Down the stretch, though, Dixon struggled, perhaps the result of tiring during a season that was much longer than what he was accustomed to. Even as his performance waned, however, Dixon continued to make an impression on Francis, who told Williams that he thought Dixon was one of the few players who worked as hard as Francis himself did.

"That's a pretty good recommendation," said Williams, who makes it clear to players that work ethic is perhaps the trait he values most.

Williams also knew that Dixon wasn't scared of anybody or anything. Williams can be a difficult coach to play for. He often yells at his players in practice or in games and can be intensely hard on a single player if he deems it necessary. Some players thrive in these circumstances, responding to the coach's challenges as if to say, "*Take that, you jerk.*" Other players, though, wilt under the coach's verbal barrages, accepting Williams's criticism as truth and not fighting back.

"My coaching style is not for everyone," Williams said. "I'm not easy to play for for some guys, because they're really sensitive or whatever. I try to make them understand that this is about getting better. The other problem is some of these guys have never been yelled at. Their high school coach is afraid they'll transfer to another high school and their summer coach is afraid they'll go to another team.

"I think the guys who stay with me, though, we have a great deal of respect once it's over. I take a great deal of pride as a coach in players' improving. No matter how good they are as freshmen, I don't want them to be the same player when they leave here."

It all went back to the adage that Dean Smith had passed on to Williams twenty-five years before, when Williams was an assistant pestering Smith with questions at a clinic: "They don't all have to like you."

Dixon, though, was not bothered by his coach's ranting. Dixon knew it. His teammates knew it. Even Williams knew it.

There was one play in practice during Dixon's freshman season that showed just how fearless "The Kid" was. Williams had just finished screaming at Dixon and the team was getting ready to run an inbounds play.

"Where's the ball?" Williams demanded.

"Here!" Dixon shot back, making like a baseball pitcher and hurling the ball at Williams from the backside.

Had it not been for senior center Brian Watkins, it might have been a very ugly situation. Watkins stuck out his hands and stopped the ball, just before it popped Williams in the head.

"You throwing the ball at me?" Williams roared—stunned, but also impressed, that a freshman had the nerve to do such a thing. "You asshole!"

Later in practice, Dixon apologized to Williams. And in the locker room afterward, he told some teammates that he had no idea what he had been thinking.

But the incident certainly made an impression on the team. It became part of the Maryland—and Juan Dixon—lore. Drew Nicholas was a high school senior at the time, but like every other player, he heard the story when he joined the Terrapins. By throwing the ball, Dixon showed that "he's not going to back down from anybody, not even Coach," Nicholas said. "A lot of guys would turn their head and walk away from it, especially when you're a freshman and you've got a coach like Coach Williams."

As for Williams, he moved past the incident almost right away.

Friends, reporters, assistant coaches, and players have incurred his wrath over the years. To those who don't know him well, Williams can be very intimidating. He doesn't discriminate. Tick him off and you'll usually hear about it, often in outbursts filled with four-letter words. Those who have been around long enough, though, also know that about ten minutes after Williams finishes a tirade, he moves on; it is as though the tirade never occurred.

"I don't have a long memory," Williams said. "I've got a pretty quick fuse, but at the same time, I come down pretty quick, too. I've always been able to do that. I'm a competitor, but I'm smart enough to know you can't let a great win or a great loss affect your next game."

If the ball-throwing incident didn't anger the coach long, it did show him what kind of player he had in Juan Dixon. Williams, in fact, likes it when players stand up to him, and Dixon had shown that he wouldn't be one of those who back down. "I haven't been able to scare Juan," Williams said. "You usually are able to scare some guys. You've got to yell at him sometimes. The thing with Juan is you never have to try to get him up, but every once in a while you have to try to get him down. Whatever I say, he doesn't take personally and he comes right back at you."

• • •

Lonny Baxter, like Dixon, wasn't expected by outsiders to be much of a contributor at an ACC school. He attended three different high schools, then spent a year at Hargrave Military Academy in south-central Virginia to improve his academics and qualify for an athletic scholarship. He was pudgy, his frame more like that a football lineman who had yet to hit the weight room than that of a basketball center.

Baxter didn't play as much as Dixon in the early going of their first year, but down the stretch, he was thrust into the starting lineup after Obinna Ekezie ruptured his Achilles tendon in practice. "I think he used that time to really learn what was expected," Williams said. "From that point on, he was a maniac in terms of work and effort."

The season ended with the disappointing loss to St. John's in the Sweet Sixteen, but as Dixon and Baxter returned for their sophomore season, they were penciled in to the starting five, though few knew what lay ahead.

As sophomores, Dixon and Baxter began to emerge as potential standouts. Francis had decided to skip his senior season and was the second overall pick in the NBA draft. Seeing just how highly Francis was regarded gave Dixon enormous confidence. Dixon knew he had fared well against Francis in practice, and if Steve was drafted so quickly, how many players still in college were as good as Francis?

Dixon hit the game-winning shot in a December victory over Illinois and was a standout in conference play, scoring more than thirty points in three different games. He led the ACC in steals and was second in scoring.

Baxter, meanwhile, was getting the job done inside, even though he had yet to develop his left hand. It had to drive opposing coaches nuts. Baxter went to his right almost every time he got the ball and he liked to use the backboard. It was as predictable as the referee throwing the ball in the air for the opening tip. Since most of the league's centers were taller than Baxter, who is only a hair above 6-6, you would figure that he would have had a hard time getting off his predictable shots.

Somehow, though, Baxter was able to do it. He was skillful at using his wide body to create space. If needed, he also would give a slight push with his left arm and avoid getting called for a foul. Baxter was used to going against taller people and knew how to be creative.

Dixon and Baxter were named first-team All-ACC as sophomores, and the future looked incredibly bright for the Terrapins.

Only the following summer, though, did Maryland realize it had a budding superstar in Dixon. One night during Gary Williams's annual summer camp, it became obvious that Dixon wasn't just good; he had the potential to be great.

The nightly games during camp feature Maryland's current and former players, as well as current and former players from other colleges and some NBA players with ties to the area. On this night, Francis was back in town after sharing NBA Rookie of the Year honors. But "Stevie Franchise," as he had become known while playing for the Houston Rockets, wasn't the best player on the court; Dixon was.

"That's when I thought in the back of my mind, 'That's what we need, a guy who's going to be good 99 percent of the games,'" assistant coach Dave Dickerson said. "In college basketball you win with a certain type of player. You always win with a player like Juan Dixon. He brings it every day and he can make shots every day.

"Juan has always made shots, against anyone or anything. He's made shots and he's taken shots. [And] he's always been resourceful. Most resourceful player I've ever coached or been around. He'll find a way. And if he can't get it done on the floor, he'll get it done with his mouth or his charm or his wit. He's resourceful. That trait helped him to be the player that he is today."

• • •

As Dixon began to emerge as a full-blown superstar as a junior, Baxter remained Mr. Consistent. He was a force inside, bulling his way to baskets and using his sleeker body to get past some of the bigger brutes he often was matched against.

Baxter's commitment to strength-and-conditioning coach Kurtis Shultz's program had paid off. He had become a conditioning addict, always lifting weights and running. He remained around 260 pounds, but had revamped his body, trading in the baby fat for muscle. Baxter had started eating better, too. Red meats and breakfasts of eggs and sausage with gravy were gone (though he still had a sweet tooth and kept eating his Frosted Flakes); he often drew curious stares as he walked down the aisles in Shoppers Food Warehouse, filling his shopping cart with oatmeal, already-cooked chicken, and vegetables.

Baxter had become leaner, stronger, and quicker, and he motivated other players with his hard work.

"When you're coaching, and I think all coaches realize it though they don't always admit it, you have to have a certain level of talent," Williams said. "Once you get past that, you want guys like Lonny Baxter, showing up every day, wanting to get better. It wasn't a matter of me pushing Lonny. It's Lonny coming in every day and kicking everybody's ass in practice. You never expect perfection. The only perfection I expect is the same effort in practice every day."

Baxter and Dixon evolved into Maryland's leaders during the 2000–01 season. Baxter was the first option on offense on the inside and Dixon the first on the outside. The Terrapins challenged Duke for supremacy in the ACC, then enjoyed the best postseason in school history. There was the oh-so-sweet victory over Georgetown in the Round of Sixteen—with Dixon besting best friend Kevin Braswell—and an 87–73 thumping of top-seeded Stanford in the West Region final, in which Baxter made eleven of eighteen shots to be named the region's most outstanding player.

"The thing with Lonny was Lonny's quickness really increased," Williams said. His new body type "not only made him stronger, but quicker. Because he still looked big when he played against the [7-foot] Collinses at Stanford and against Georgetown. They said, 'He is only 6-8,' but didn't realize how quick he was.

"It always amazed me about Lonny Baxter, every game he had to prove himself. It wasn't good enough that he beat Georgetown's and Stanford's front lines," he had to do it again as a senior.

Dixon had proven himself, again leading the team in scoring and the ACC in steals; for the second consecutive season he earned first-team All-ACC honors. Still, he continued to push himself, refusing to be content with his game. Even when his teammates were tired of basketball and wanting to rest their legs, Dixon was getting into Cole for extra work, dragging along whomever he could find to rebound.

"Three or four nights during the week, he's probably in the gym shooting," Drew Nicholas said. "That's a lot. You get tired. You go through periods in the year where your body goes and you're fighting to get through practice to get ready for the game."

Dixon was highly competitive, whether it was with teammates or opponents. In practice or pickup games, he would get all over teammates. In games, he would do anything necessary, whether it meant going all out for a loose ball or ignoring leg cramps to chase after an opponent. "That usually doesn't happen when you have a guy who knows he's an All-American," Tahj Holden said.

Dixon's teammates also marveled at his neatness. His bedroom was immaculate. His bathroom was spotless, with plenty of cleaning supplies in the vanity under the sink. Dixon's laundry was neatly folded, his closet and dresser orderly. Empty shoe boxes were stacked in one corner; if there was one habit Dixon couldn't kick, it was his fondness for shoes. If dishes were left in the kitchen sink, Dixon cleaned them, then made it clear to his roommates that such behavior was unacceptable. If there was anything in the trash can, it was emptied.

Calling Juan Dixon a neat freak was putting it mildly.

"He takes it to the next level," said Earl Badu, one of Dixon's close friends and roommates. "Cleaning things that have already been cleaned."

Badu talked about the time Dixon saw a television ad for a cleaning glove. Two days later, Badu said, a similar glove resided under the kitchen sink.

"This is me," Dixon said one day, showing off the spotless quarters that he considered his sanctuary. "Neat and organized."

If Dixon stood out with his cleanliness, in other respects he was quite normal. He loved watching basketball games on TV and discussing them with his roommates, Drew Nicholas, Earl Badu, and team manager Brian Cavanaugh. Dixon also was among the many players who enjoyed watching late-night dating shows with catchy names such as *Blind Date, The Fifth Wheel,* and *Elimidate,* laughing at some of the stunts pulled by the guys on the shows.

Over time, Dixon had become one of the team's most outgoing players. As a freshman, he was incredibly quiet, rarely speaking up, Williams remembered. By the time Dixon was a junior, however, he was comfortable in any setting, from talking with older boosters to handling the way children looked up to him and answering their questions. He signed hundreds of autographs, but his cursive signature rarely changed, almost always nice and neat with a "#3" tucked inside.

"It's crazy," Dixon said. "But I don't really have a chance to think about it. I never imagined it would be like this. This is what comes with fame. If you're a known athlete, you are going to have to pay your dues. I guess that's a part of paying your dues."

"Not everybody can do that," Williams said of how Dixon handled the attention. "It's not necessarily fair for you to have to do that when you're twenty-two, but in Juan's career, he got placed into that leadership on campus. Juan was the most famous student here by his senior year.

"Juan had the patience to do the media things that he had to do in addition to the time you put in with normal basketball stuff. Juan always had the ability to juggle that. With some guys, you always worried about how much talking they did to the media, that they were going to get a big head and not practice well. Juan proved how good he is in those situations.

"I've got friends who would bring their kids or grandkids to practice, and at the end of practice the father will push the kid out on the court to talk to Juan, and Juan will wind up shooting with him. There was a time in Juan's life, looking back now, where he probably felt he didn't get the attention paid to him by adults. Now it looks like whenever he is in that situation, he makes sure the kid felt he got the attention from Juan Dixon. And I think that's important to Juan."

Still, while Dixon was willing to give part of himself to outsiders—shaking hands, smiling for pictures, and signing autographs—he also maintained a careful distance.

"People think they know Juan and see him being very sociable and open, but he has his private side," Williams said. "When he's out, he's on and very friendly and a good guy. But he keeps his space, too.... There's not an immediate trust with anything when you grow up like [Juan did], I would think. You always have that ability, before you let yourself become totally open to somebody—it's like an invisible barrier there."

Dixon also had his superstitions, reshowering and brushing his hair just before games, as if that somehow would affect his three-point shooting. His clothes had to be laid out neatly in his locker. Everything had to be just perfect—the way he had been brought up.

"I think that my parents' dying definitely made me stronger," Dixon said. "I think I do have an edge when I step on the court, because you always have to believe in yourself. And I believe."

CHAPTER 5

"Maybe It's Just a Lot of Hype"

It was eerily quiet. None of the players knew quite what to say. And Coach Gary Williams could not say, would not say, what first came to his mind.

At first glance, this had been a game Maryland was supposed to win easily. After all, the Terrapins were the nation's second-ranked team. And their opponent was mostly a bunch of kids just a few months removed from high school.

But having spent months talking about being ready for opponents' best shots and not taking anyone lightly, the Terrapins were outhustled and outplayed at seemingly every position by younger, smaller, less-heralded opponents. Making things worse, since none of the nation's other teams were playing, many were in the dorm rooms or apartments watching not-so-mighty Maryland get beaten by unranked Arizona, 71–67, in the Coaches vs. Cancer Classic in New York's Madison Square Garden.

"We came in there and we knew we were the better team. We showed up knowing we were going to win and we didn't," forward Byron Mouton said. "Even though we were a top-five team, that doesn't give us the right to just win the game. We realized there was a lot of stuff to do.

"Ain't no way we're supposed to lose that game."

But they did. The game plan for the earliest season opener in school history, on November 8, had been simple. Get out in transition. Force the tempo. Take advantage of Arizona's inexperience—the Wildcats' lineup had two freshmen in the starting five, a total of four in the top seven, as Arizona was not in the national rankings for the first time in more than eleven years. Blow out the Wildcats early, don't give them any hope. Celebrate briefly and start thinking about a showdown with fifth-ranked Florida in Friday's championship, the game everyone was waiting for.

Yep, that was what the opening night of the college basketball season was supposed to hold for the nation's second-ranked team, one that had set its sights on a national championship.

Naturally, none of it happened.

And so less than five hours into the college basketball season, the Maryland Terrapins were 0–1.

Inside, Williams was irate as he and his players shook hands with the victorious Wildcats, whose gleeful smiles and hugs showed this was not just any old early-season victory.

Williams demands effort. It's Priority Number One, Two, and Three. But the Terrapins had penciled in a "W" before even taking the court.

How could they do this? How could the players just waltz in thinking they were going to win?

Didn't they listen? Hadn't they paid attention? Didn't they hear the warnings that everybody was going to be fired up to play big bad Maryland after its Final Four appearance?

"Our thing was, it's almost impossible, but it was to have a perfect season. We wanted to be perfect," Mouton said. "No matter what, Duke is always the team to beat. We wanted to be on the same level with them. And Kansas. But by losing that game [to Arizona], to a young team, a lot of people had second thoughts about Maryland. 'Maybe it's just a lot of hype.' "

There certainly wasn't an abundance of substance. The game was like most college basketball games in November: sloppy, with little consistency other than turnovers and missed shots. Perhaps it was the result of all the anticipation, the extra adrenaline that was easy to spot before the game.

"It was real intense," said point guard Steve Blake, who had become acquainted with a handful of Arizona players, including point guard Jason Gardner, the Wildcats' best player, at a basketball camp the previous summer.

"I kept telling the guys they could play. I knew they were going to be good. Of course, I wanted to outplay [Gardner], but as long as we win, the individual matchup doesn't matter."

● ● ●

The season's first basket had been a fast-break dunk by Chris Wilcox off a feed from Juan Dixon, after Dixon made a steal. It was the kind of play Maryland's players had grown to expect from Wilcox; in full stride he took the pass between the NBA and college three-point lines and took two steps before powerfully slamming the ball through the rim with his right hand. The harder you slam it, the more points you get, it seemed Wilcox thought.

For a while, things seemed to go according to plan. When Mouton threw a pass over Arizona's zone defense and Dixon easily made a three-pointer from the right wing, the lead was 20–13. This was how it was supposed to be.

But Arizona came right back. Freshman Salim Stoudamire made a three-pointer, and then Gardner—the only starter back from the team that had lost to Duke in the NCAA final—stole a pass by Blake and made an uncontested layup to make it 20–20.

The Terrapins were trying hard, but the mistakes kept piling up. Drew Nicholas, an excellent shooter, missed a pair of free throws, rebounded the second miss, and scored while being fouled. He missed another free throw—something that soon would become a painful habit for the Terrapins—and Baxter grabbed that rebound but lost the ball out of bounds.

A few minutes later, just after making his third three-pointer, Dixon was called for an offensive foul, for using a forearm to push off and separate himself from a defender. Williams followed his standard procedure, taking Dixon out of the game because he had two fouls. As he sat on the bench, Dixon angrily punched his right fist into the palm of his left hand—clearly upset with himself, because he knew his presence was vital.

At the half, it was tied at 33.

The team headed to the locker room, with Williams and his assistants a few steps behind. As is his routine, Williams took a towel and a water bottle from one of the team's student managers as he entered the locker room. And as usual, it was only a matter of seconds before he flung the bottle in a fit of rage.

The message at halftime was fairly standard. Focus. Rebound. And stop missing those free throws.

The Terrapins got a good start to the second half when Wilcox posted up for a short bank shot, but then Dixon was called for his third foul, on a silly attempt to try to strip the ball from Arizona freshman center Isaiah Fox.

"God!" Dixon screamed at himself as he clasped his hands in front of his body, realizing his mistake.

It was the kind of play a poised veteran is not supposed to make, especially when he knows his importance to the team. With three fouls,

Dixon was only two fouls away from being disqualified, and with so much time remaining, he was forced to go to the bench. Sitting on the sidelines with a towel around his neck, he was little more than a glorified cheerleader, reduced to trying to point things out to the players on the floor. Without the unnecessary reach-in or the first-half push-off, Dixon could have stayed on the floor.

Arizona built a small lead, but Maryland stayed close, and Blake's first basket of the season, a three-pointer from the left wing, tied it at 45. Every time Maryland scored, the Terrapins seemed to feel that this was the time Arizona would crumple and they would take control.

But the Wildcats scored the next eight points, and it was 53–45 midway through the half. Maryland had scored twelve points in ten minutes. So much for forcing the tempo and being the aggressor.

"Arizona wants it more!" Williams screamed at no one in particular.

Maybe that made a difference. Dixon, who had been on the bench with his three fouls, returned and made a pair of three-pointers. Wilcox threw an alley-oop pass to Baxter, who dunked and then waved his arms in the air, imploring a contingent of Maryland fans to get louder. Then Dixon made a steal and Maryland had a four-on-two fast break. But instead of attacking the basket as he normally might, Dixon coolly passed to Blake alone in the left corner, and his three-pointer put Maryland back in front, 56–55. It was a very confident play, the team's leading scorer passing up a chance to attack in favor of getting a dagger that might finally get the younger Wildcats to go away.

And when Nicholas passed to Baxter for a bank shot from the right side, Maryland's lead was 58–55.

That quickly, Maryland had shown why it was regarded so highly. The Terrapins had been sleepwalking, but seemingly with the flip of a switch they had rattled off a 13–2 run.

Just as quickly, though, Dixon picked up his fourth foul, another one he could have avoided, as he tried to defend Gardner far from the basket.

With 5:14 left, again he went to the bench, pulling his jersey up over his face in disgust with himself.

Sure enough, with Dixon back on the bench, Maryland was unable to hold its lead. A minute later, Gardner made two free throws, and then Rick Anderson, who had sat out the previous season because he would have played little, made a runner in the lane. It was 61–60, Arizona.

Finally, with 3:17 left, came the decisive play. Gardner, wide open on the left wing, made a three-pointer as he was knocked on his rear end by Baxter, who had tried to close quickly and instead of a block got a foul. Gardner's subsequent free throw made it 65–61.

Dixon returned and banked in a runner in traffic, and then Baxter drew a charge; Maryland had the ball back and a chance to tie, or even take the lead with a three-pointer. But there was not going to be a comeback. With the shot clock just under ten seconds, Blake hurried a three-pointer from the top of the key and it wasn't close.

At the other end, Arizona freshman Will Bynum wildly drove to the basket and lost the ball. As Bynum and Blake tumbled to the floor and the ball went through the hoop, everyone turned to see what the call would be. . . . A blocking foul on Blake, count the basket, 67–63.

Bynum missed the free throw, and Nicholas found Wilcox for a short basket. Maryland was within two points, 67–65, with close to two minutes left—plenty of time.

"Do you want it?" Williams bellowed as Arizona called a timeout after getting two offensive rebounds but failing to score.

Baxter and Blake combined to block a shot by Gardner, and then Isaiah Fox had his close shot deflected by Baxter. Fox, though, persevered, grabbing the rebound and scoring.

With the game on the line, Maryland had allowed four offensive rebounds on one possession. One possession! Williams was incensed as he called a timeout with forty-two seconds left. What was going on?

Dixon missed a long three-pointer, but Maryland got the ball back when Gardner was called for traveling. Dixon and Blake missed; finally, Wilcox made a jumper from the left side to bring the Terrapins back within two, 69–67, with 4.6 seconds left.

Maryland fouled Rick Anderson on the ensuing play. Anderson made both of his free throws and it was 71–67 with three seconds left. The game was over.

Less than forty-eight hours earlier, Williams and the tournament's other three head coaches had rung the closing bell at the New York Stock Exchange. Now he was thinking about mind games. And the only thing worse than being 0–1, he knew, was being 0–2 with a four-hour bus ride ahead. So the players were spared a verbal barrage. Williams, often caught by television cameras with a red face as he berated his players, suppressed his anger. Mentally beating the players up would do no good, he realized, not when they had less than twenty-four hours to prepare for the consolation game against Temple, a team that forced opponents to play its grinding style.

It was quite a change from the past, when Williams almost certainly would have gone on a rampage after such a disappointing performance.

"I think the biggest change I've seen in him was that he realized the cup was half full instead of being half empty," said Dave Dickerson, who was in his sixth year as an assistant coach for Williams. "Each team is different from year to year. And certain teams you have to handle differently. Some teams you can talk to and they realize they screwed up. Some teams you have to make them understand they screwed up. And some teams you don't have to say anything to. . . .

"Yeah, he was disappointed. But being an experienced coach and being a smart person, he knew that game didn't make the season. No one has won or lost a national championship in November, I don't think."

The players got the message.

"Coach Williams made sure [the team felt] that yes, it was a loss, but we're not trying to be 0–2 here," Nicholas said.

"I could tell the difference," Mouton said. "Every year it seemed he was getting calmer and calmer. He picked his points to yell at us. Everybody was talking about how Arizona was a young team. But he said, 'They're not a young team, they're a good team. At the end of the year, they're going to be in the tournament.'"

He was right; when all was said and done, Arizona would finish tied for second in the Pac-10 Conference and advance to the NCAA tournament Round of Sixteen.

For now, only a few hours into the season, Arizona still was the team that nobody knew or expected anything from.

"We were set up," Williams said in retrospect. "There were [future] pros on that team, [junior Luke] Walton and the other big guy inside. That was the first game we played since Duke in the Final Four—there was a little residue there, I'm sure. That was a tough loss, but you've got to get that out of your system.

"It's easy to look back, but it was almost a good thing, because everybody was saying how good we were. Then you lose and it's, 'Damn, we're not that good.'... Maybe if we win that game, we don't [have the same desire]."

• • •

By this time, Williams had talked—and seen—enough of Arizona. By losing its opening game, Maryland was stuck in the 6:30 P.M. consolation game on Friday. Assistant coaches Dickerson, Jimmy Patsos, and Matt Kovarik had scouted Florida's 72–64 victory over Temple, fully expecting to play the fifth-ranked Gators, who liked to play at a fast tempo with their wealth of talented players.

Now the coaching staff walked across the street to the hotel, told the team managers to get them some food, and retreated to Williams's room for a four-hour powwow to devise a game plan for Temple, often considered one of the most difficult teams to play against because of its tenacious defense. It was past 3 A.M. by the time the coaches went to sleep.

With little time to prepare, Williams was focused Friday morning when the Terrapins walked to the Garden for the team's shootaround. The smiling, joking, and laughing that had been present a day before, when everyone was supremely confident, was nowhere to be found as Williams talked about making the extra pass and moving the ball around the court against Temple's matchup zone defense.

"Guys were a lot more focused," Nicholas said. "We had just lost, so we were waiting around to see how Coach was going to react. And there wasn't too much joking around, put it that way. We knew he's never been tough on game days, because we've got to play that night. But he was stern with the things he wanted to emphasize. He wanted to get his things across."

Those things weren't much of a surprise. Get the ball inside to Baxter. Don't go four of twelve from the foul line again. Rebound better. That last series of rebounds was particularly bothersome. How could Maryland's experienced players have let a freshman outwork them in such a critical situation?

In addition to the strategic emphasis, Williams made one noticeable change, putting Holden in the starting lineup and bringing Wilcox off the bench.

"I thought for sure [Wilcox] would start, but we just seemed to play better early with Tahj in there," Williams said. "Gradually, as you play good teams, you realize the athletic ability Chris could give you" off the bench.

It probably was not a coincidence that after Arizona pushed the Terrapins around, Williams chose to insert Holden into the starting five. Holden had arrived with a reputation for being soft, not as physical as a man his size should be. In his first two seasons, however, Holden had dispelled that notion. He had proven to be one of the toughest players on the team, willing to do anything to get the job done, raising his shoulders and elbows without a second thought.

"I think I got a bad rap because I had the ability to shoot," Holden said. "When you're 6-10, there are not a lot of guys in high school who have that ability. In my high school, I was lucky enough to have another guy who was a really good power forward, so I could play outside. Plus, I was so much bigger than everybody in my league that [if] I bumped into a guy, it was a foul on me because I was so much bigger."

But in the early minutes against Temple, it didn't matter whether Holden or Wilcox was starting at power forward; nothing seemed to go right. Owls freshman Nile Murry started the game with a three-pointer. Baxter missed inside, and then Blake's pass for Mouton was off the mark and wound up in the lap of a front-row fan. The Terrapins were trying to force things, trying to do too much too soon. Temple beat Maryland's press for one basket, then another, the second coming when hefty Ron Rollerson was fouled as he tried to dunk and the ball rattled in anyway.

It was a miserable start for the Terrapins, who trailed 10–2.

Whether it was a lack of energy or a lack of composure, Williams sensed things were wrong and soon inserted seldom-used forward Calvin McCall into the game, hoping the presence of the former football quarterback would give the Terrapins a spark.

And within a few minutes, Maryland was back in the game. Blake found Holden for a three-point play, and Baxter scored on a put-back. Nicholas dribbled into the paint and passed to Dixon for an open three-pointer from the right side, the kind of shot that was like a layup for Dixon. It seemed so smooth and simple—play hard, make smart passes, sink open shots.

Dixon made a running shot from the left side, and then Nicholas found Wilcox for a jump hook. Nicholas to Dixon for a jumper in transition. Mouton, having returned for McCall, for three from the left side. A 22–15 Maryland lead.

Of course, the lead didn't hold up. Temple guard Brian Polk made his third three-pointer, and Rollerson posted up for a bucket to put Temple back in front, 26–25.

Williams called timeout. Maryland was shooting the ball with great accuracy, having made ten of fifteen shots against the Owls' acclaimed matchup zone defense—and the Terrapins were losing!

It didn't get better immediately. Dixon had a shot blocked, and then Temple's other beefy inside player, Kevin Lyde, scored on a third-chance tip-in. After a bad pass by McCall, Lynn Greer was fouled and made two free throws for a 30–25 Temple lead.

With the tension building, Dixon did not let his teammates down. He made a three-pointer from the right wing, then one from the left corner to tie it at 32, though he appeared to injure his ankle. No matter. Dixon forced Greer into taking a bad shot, then went to the other end and made another three-pointer, this one from the left side. In a sign of things to come later in the season, the Terrapins had turned it on, closing the half with a 14–2 run to take a 39–32 lead.

Temple got close a few times in the second half, but Maryland had a response each time. The final score was 82–74. Maryland finished twenty-six of forty-four from the field, including a splendid twelve of nineteen from three-point range. Dixon led the way with twenty-five points. Things certainly seemed better than they had only a few hours earlier, as the Terrapins had avoided losing their opening two games for the first time since 1962.

"That was real important," Nicholas said. "We had to gain back some confidence. We knew Temple was a good basketball team. So we had to go out and get a win. We were so up from the preseason polls, the hype, and the media and everyone telling us we were in the top five. You're not supposed to go out and lose your season opener to a bunch of freshmen. I don't think we lost our confidence, but we woke up a little bit. We just realized that we needed to step up and play."

Going 1–1 wasn't ideal, but it sure beat the previous season, when Maryland opened on the picturesque isle of Maui and lost two of three games. That year, after the Terrapins lost to Dayton in a consolation game to wrap up the tournament, Williams had skipped the team bus ride and walked the two miles back to the hotel.

Now Williams simply walked out of the locker room and boarded the team's charter bus. While Florida and Arizona played in the championship game, Maryland's bus rolled through the darkness and down the New Jersey Turnpike, everybody chirping away, including Williams, who was telling stories about his days in Collingswood as the bus passed his hometown. And for those on board, there was at least one pleasant thought: the Maryland Terrapins had averted the embarrassment of being 0–2. On this night, that was more than enough to feel good about.

"It was a great win for us because the doubters had been out there very quickly," Williams said. "It took a lot of Maryland fans until about after we were able to shake hands with Arizona and walking out of there to start saying negative things about our team. I don't hear much during the game, but after the game, I hear a lot of things."

It was also beneficial that for one of the few times this season, Maryland played on consecutive nights, giving the team a quick chance to make another impression. "If we had a lot of time in between, we might have been sulking and been real disappointed for a while," Blake said. "Because we played well against Temple, it let us feel good about ourselves."

• • •

A few hours after the team bus pulled behind Cole Field House, assistant coach Dave Dickerson was at the airport, flying to South Carolina. Crazy travel schedules are not unusual for coaches, who often have to cram in recruiting trips whenever possible.

But this was a different trip. On the morning before the season opener, Dickerson's cell phone had rung with the news that his father had passed away after a short bout with cancer.

After Maryland's run to the 2001 Final Four, Dave Sr. had learned that he had liver and lung cancer; doctors had given him only three to six months to live. Dave Jr. had made several trips back and forth to his parents' home in Olar, South Carolina, wanting to spend as much time as possible with his father.

"I was his only son," said Dickerson, who has six older sisters. "I felt bad about the situation. He always wanted me to take a job closer to home or in South Carolina or at the University of South Carolina. We were close. We were as close as a father and son could get. I love my father, but I respected him more. He was the authority in my life. It was one of those things where we were close, but I was scared of him also. One of those things where I may be talking loud in a room and having fun, and my father walked in and you had to get yourself together.

"My father was a baseball fanatic. My only regret with being his son was that I didn't play baseball. That was the sport he understood and loved and he played when he was young."

Born and raised in South Carolina, Dave Dickerson had his eyes set on a different part of the country. A slim, 6-foot-6-inch forward, he had scholarship offers from the Palmetto State's top two programs, the South Carolina Gamecocks and the Clemson Tigers, as well as from Memphis State, Miami (Florida), Georgia, and Maryland. Growing up in the South, Dickerson knew the powerful pull of Atlantic Coast Conference basketball and was eager to play in the league.

"I came to Maryland for two reasons," he said. "I wanted to play in the ACC and I wanted to get out of the South. Maryland was the northern school in the ACC and it wasn't in the South."

After playing at Maryland, Dickerson stayed at the school for one more year to earn his degree in government and politics. That was Gary

Williams's first season as the team's head coach, and Dickerson stopped by the coaches' office to introduce himself early in the school year; occasionally he attended practice. One day the following summer, after graduation, Dickerson approached Williams on the Cole Field House floor to tell the coach he had gotten a job as an assistant coach at Gardner-Webb College in Boiling Springs, North Carolina.

"'Make sure you like it,'" Dickerson remembered Williams saying. "He never asked me how it was going. It was always, 'Do you like it? How is it going for you?' I think he knew that coaching is something you've got to do because you like it. You've got to love it. If you don't, you spend too much damn time doing it."

The two kept in touch over the years, often exchanging notes as Dickerson spent one season at Gardner-Webb, one season at James Madison University in Harrisonburg, Virginia, and four more as an assistant at Radford University in southwestern Virginia. And in 1996, when Williams let assistant Art Perry go, he turned to Dickerson.

Dickerson never did go back to South Carolina, and with the demands of the job—both during the season and in the off-season, because of recruiting—it was a challenge to make time to go home. By the time Maryland traveled to New York to open the 2001–02 season, Dickerson knew the end was near for his father. He had spoken to Dave Sr. that Monday, and the team departed on Tuesday. On Wednesday morning, around 6:30, he already was awake when his phone rang.

"I was prepared," Dickerson said. "The easiest way to deal with anything is being prepared. So I was prepared for that. And it wasn't as bad as if it had been two years before. I was just fortunate and happy that he wasn't suffering at the time. He was just getting to the stage where he would have really suffered."

With that in mind, Dickerson stayed with the team through its games, then flew with his wife, Laurette, and son, Dave III, to South Carolina on Saturday. The funeral was Sunday and Dickerson returned on Tuesday.

• • •

The final home opener in the history of Cole Field House came on November 17, when American University, coached by former Virginia coach Jeff Jones, made the brief trip from Washington to College Park.

The Saturday afternoon began with the unveiling of a banner above midcourt to commemorate the team's Final Four run of the previous season. It was a happy moment, but also one that stoked memories of just how close the Terrapins had come to going all the way.

Once the game started, Maryland took a quick 12–6 lead, then scored fifteen consecutive points to put the game out of reach. It was the part of a season-long trend that would see the Terrapins do much of their damage in quick bursts.

"Teams like that will stay with you the first five minutes and everybody is like, 'What's going on?'" Blake said. "Then, bam, we go on a 20–0 run. I think it's expected to beat [teams like American] by thirty. We expect to, too. It's a letdown if we don't."

With the 83–53 victory, Williams became the second-winningest coach in school history, passing his own former coach, Bud Millikan. "Coach Millikan would have more wins if he didn't play me," Williams joked.

A 77–53 victory over Delaware State followed, and then the fifth-ranked Terrapins got another chance in the spotlight with second-ranked Illinois coming to Cole on November 27 as part of the ACC/Big Ten Challenge.

In the days leading up to the Illinois game, Gary Williams made sure that some of the annual preseason magazines made their way into the locker room. Illinois was talented, particularly in the backcourt, where the tandem of point guard Frank Williams and shooting guard Cory Bradford was considered one of the best, if not the best, in the nation.

"You know, Juan and Blake, they certainly took notice of the rankings," Williams said. But the coach wryly avoided taking responsibility for the mind game. "The magazines just seem to make their way into the locker room. It was a chance for the media to read those magazines in case they missed it."

The players definitely got the message, particularly since they pretty much had bombed in their season debut against Arizona, leaving themselves open for questioning. Illinois represented a chance for redemption, a game against a top opponent on national television. It didn't hurt that the previous season, in Maui, the Fighting Illini had pushed Maryland all over the court in a 90–80 victory.

"We were definitely getting up for this game," Blake said. "It was our time to prove ourselves again, that we were one of the elite teams in the country. Myself, going up against Frank Williams—it gets you excited. That's all you think about, how we're going to get ready for that game. It's in your mind constantly, even when you're sitting in class."

It was a tough ticket, perhaps second only to Duke in terms of difficulty. Cole, as always for big games, would be hot and stuffy, prompting the Terrapins to drink more water than usual to stay hydrated as they faced the toughest test to their seventy-nine-game nonconference home winning streak. The atmosphere was electric, and Maryland's play only made the crowd get louder. Chris Wilcox came off the bench to dominate inside, making eight of thirteen shots and scoring nineteen points. Dixon poured in twenty-five. After falling behind 17–10, Maryland took control with a 12–0 run and went to halftime with a 41–29 lead.

From there, the lead only grew bigger. A 10–2 run to open the second half made it 51–31, and Maryland cruised to a 76–63 victory. The Terrapins had reestablished themselves. Blake and Dixon had combined for thirty-five points and helped hold Williams and Bradford to eighteen on seven-of-thirty shooting.

"Then you've got to calm them down," Gary Williams said. "People think that only after a loss it's a tough job. But you win on national television and beat the number-two team in the country, all the students are telling them how great they are. The next day you practice, you have to make sure they understand this is November—let's calm down, we've got thirty more games, hopefully.

"Our players understood the meaning of we've got to get better. It's not that we're not good, but all good teams have to improve. Whatever we were against Illinois, that won't be good enough to beat Duke in February. Players always want to believe they've made it and they don't have to work anymore. But that's not true. Hopefully, you get to March and you've maxed out where you can get as a team and can sustain it as long as you can.

"The great thing about coaching is you can always get better, not only as a basketball coach but as a motivator. You try to push the right buttons with players.... We're not going to play perfect and I'm not going to coach perfect, but I'm going to coach my ass off and I expect you guys to play the same way. Coaches make mistakes. You call a wrong play and look back after the game: 'What was I thinking about?'

"You get a timeout once in a while, that's when you've got to have the right play set. Know the time and situation—there's no excuse for not running the correct play. When you're on your game as a coach, you go situation to situation and make all the right decisions. You know after the game whether you did it or not."

On this Tuesday night, a month before Christmas, Williams—and the Terrapins—had come pretty close.

CHAPTER 6

A Long December

Washington is a basketball town. The Redskins might be king of the nation's capital, but it is basketball that captures the city, from the playgrounds, to the high schools, to the colleges, to that NBA team that brought Michael Jordan out of retirement.

There is the tradition of stars like Elgin Baylor and Dave Bing. Morgan Wootten built DeMatha High into a national powerhouse with players including Adrian Dantley and Danny Ferry. The Washington Bullets had their glory years, winning the NBA title in 1978 led by an undersized center named Wes Unseld. John Thompson guided Georgetown University to national prominence. Red Auerbach, who led the Boston Celtics to greatness, calls Washington home.

The city's heart beats like a bouncing basketball.

But there is no signature basketball event in Washington.

In fact, before His Airness came along, for some folks the annual City Title high school basketball game might have been the biggest game in the city. The Wizards made the NBA playoffs just once between 1985 and 2002, getting swept in the first round in 1997.

Though Washington has a bunch of colleges, it has no headline games. The Big East Conference tournament is played in New York City. The Atlantic Coast Conference tournament has been held in North Carolina in forty-four of its first forty-nine years. Even the midlevel conferences with teams in the region go elsewhere: the Atlantic 10 tournament is in Philadelphia, the Colonial in Richmond.

Philadelphia, just a few miles from where Gary Williams grew up, had the Palestra and weekend doubleheaders. Georgetown and Maryland, the Washington area's top two teams, met just once in the regular season after 1980. In the country's most political city, politics rule on the hardwood.

In recent years, though, Washington has had the BB&T Classic, which, while it doesn't command a heap of star power, does bring together Maryland, George Washington, and two nationally known teams for a tournament one weekend in early December.

For the Terrapins, the event has provided some memorable victories. In 1997, the fourth year of the event, the Terrapins beat second-ranked Kansas, then lost to GW in the championship game. In 1998, number-two Maryland beat number-five Stanford.

In the 2001 BB&T, Maryland and GW were joined by Connecticut and Princeton. In a change from seasons past, Maryland was matched against the perceived lesser opponent in the opening round, Princeton. That allowed GW's new coach, Karl Hobbs, to face his former boss, Connecticut coach Jim Calhoun.

Pete Carril, who looked every bit the Ivy League professor with his gray hair flying in all directions, was no longer Princeton's coach, having retired and been replaced by John Thompson III. The Tigers, though, remained the same team they had been under Carril, running the same back-door plays over and over and over, and running opponents into submission with their patient play.

It was the same offense with which Princeton had upset defending national champion UCLA in the first round of the 1996 NCAA tournament and nearly knocked off number-one seed Georgetown in the first round of the 1989 NCAA tournament. Those teams, like Maryland, were supposed to have players that were bigger, stronger, faster, and just plain better than Princeton's, capable of routing the Ivy Leaguers with ease.

Of course, what is supposed to happen and what actually happens are two different things. And at halftime of the BB&T tournament's opening game, Maryland, whose fans outnumbered everyone else in the building by about a three-to-one margin, was booed heartily. The Terrapins trailed 36–23 and had twelve turnovers and only seven baskets.

In the locker room, Coach Williams went ballistic. "These guys are supposed to not be big-time players," point guard Steve Blake said. Williams "couldn't be too happy with the way we were playing. . . . He laid into us. It's embarrassing when you get beat on a back-door cut even though everybody knows they're going to do it."

Said Byron Mouton, "It was almost funny, because we were trying so hard and we couldn't do anything. We couldn't stop them. It was so weird, because they're not athletic or running plays that we couldn't stop. That was the sad thing. It's the most frustrating thing when even though you know what they're going to do, you still can't stop it."

Like Williams, freshman forward Mike Grinnon had watched the first half from the bench. And like Williams, Grinnon couldn't believe what he was seeing. He had been recruited by Princeton but chose Maryland because of its high caliber of basketball. "I knew if I was at Princeton, I could be starting and be one of the main players," Grinnon said. "That was probably one where I had to swallow my pride the most. I'll never forget that."

Grinnon didn't have to swallow too hard, though. After falling behind by fifteen on a quick basket to start the half, Maryland chipped away at its deficit, limiting the Tigers to precious few back-door chances. With less than seven minutes left, Byron Mouton made two free throws to tie it at 46–46. Two minutes later, Juan Dixon finally got his hands on one of those pesky back-door passes, and Blake fed Drew Nicholas for a long three-pointer from straight out. That gave the Terrapins their first lead since the opening minute, 51–49, with 4:43 left. Maryland was able to hold on for its fifth consecutive victory, 61–53.

"You get a win like that and everybody knows it's a good win," Blake said. "It was very physically tiring, because you're trying to press up on them and they run around nonstop. It's exhausting, physically and mentally."

As tired as the Terrapins were, however, there was not much time to regroup. During the season, Williams often gives the team a day off following a game. Some of the players show up at the gym to work on their shots, but the coach spares them a rigid workout so they can rest their legs. This, though, would be one of three occasions when Maryland would play on consecutive days.

Maryland's opponent in the December 3 championship game was Connecticut. The Huskies had a budding star in sophomore forward Caron Butler, the twenty-one-year-old father of two who had done hard time as a juvenile but appeared to have turned his life around. Senior Johnnie Selvie was a tough and rugged power forward. UConn also had a slew of backcourt talent in freshman Ben Gordon, sophomore Taliek Brown, and junior Tony Robertson. Freshman center Emeka Okafor was quickly emerging as a top-notch shot blocker.

In short, the Huskies had all the makings of a team on the rise, with talented young players who needed to mature and gain experience.

In December, though, UConn simply could not stay with Maryland. This game seemed nothing like the season opener against Arizona, since the Terrapins now took it to their younger opponent, playing in-your-face defense and building a 21–7 lead. UConn scored the next thirteen points and for a while kept it close, but Maryland simply had too much. The final was 77–65, and center Lonny Baxter, who had twenty-four points and ten rebounds, was named the tournament's most valuable player.

• • •

The players left the court clutching all sorts of trophies: tournament MVP, all-tournament team, tournament champion. As they laughed and danced their way to the locker room for a quick change into their black warm-ups before the short bus ride back to College Park, forward Byron Mouton was approached by assistant coach Dave Dickerson.

"Go ride home with your brother," Dickerson suggested.

At first, Mouton resisted. After all, this setting was part of the fun for Mouton, being among his teammates, celebrating a feel-good victory, swaggering about, joking and playing around in the back of the bus on the ride home.

But when Dickerson persisted, Mouton agreed to ride with his older brother Clyde, who lived in Maryland.

The ride back to campus was uneventful, with the two brothers discussing the victory and how Byron had played. He had made only one of seven shots and scored just two points, but it hardly mattered. Mouton had given up his best chances to score points by the bucketful when he left Tulane and enrolled at Maryland. The way Byron looked at it, a win was a win. How else is a role player supposed to look at things?

As the car pulled up to Baltimore Hall, though, Clyde suddenly got serious.

"Something went on back home," he said, before explaining that Kevin Mouton, the second oldest of the five Mouton brothers, had been shot dead after a party in Houston.

"Man, you need to stop playing," Byron quickly shot back.

But Byron soon found out this was no joke. Kevin Mouton, thirty-two, had been found by police in the predawn hours the previous morning, his limp body slumped over the steering wheel of his car after it had crashed into two parked vehicles, according to a Houston Police Department report. The news had been kept from Mouton until after the tournament was over.

When he realized that Clyde was serious, Byron couldn't believe it. "Why did this happen to my family?" he asked himself over and over. "Something can happen, but why would somebody want to hurt my brother like that? You always read about that stuff in the newspapers and always see it on the news on TV, but never in your life do you think it is going to happen to you."

Like Byron, Kevin Mouton was outgoing, always trying to liven up a room. All the boys, including Kristhan and Brian, and their one sister, Darlene, had been close. They had spread themselves around the country, but home always was in Rayne, Louisiana, a town of ten thousand people that bills itself as the Frog Capital of the World, conjuring up all sorts of images for outsiders.

Normally, Byron looked forward to returning to Rayne, which is just off Interstate 10, midway between New Orleans and the Louisiana-Texas state line. He enjoyed horsing around with friends and going fishing. This trip, though, would be anything but enjoyable.

From the moment he got back to Rayne, Mouton was worried about his mother, Shirley, and began wondering whether it was worth going back to Maryland.

"I'm not leaving until I make sure you are all right," he said.

Shirley Mouton wanted no such talk.

"You know your brother knew you loved to play ball," she told Byron. "The best thing he wants you to do is continue what you're doing. I would love for you to stay, but if you stayed around here, nothing good would come out of it."

Dickerson arrived in time for the funeral on Saturday, and that night he and Mouton drove to New Orleans and flew back to Maryland.

"I can't imagine what he went through," said Dickerson, whose father had passed away just one month earlier. "I think the thing that helped Byron is that he has a close family. They somehow got through this thing together. We had a close team that gave him encouragement and helped him through everything.

"Byron has been one of the most courageous young men I've been around. He wanted to go to Kentucky but [Coach Rick] Pitino left, so he settled on Tulane. He probably could have stayed at Tulane two more years and scored a lot of points and won some individual awards and everything, but he gave that up to come to Maryland. Hell, I couldn't have done that. If I could have shot the ball twenty-five times a game, I would have stayed at that school."

Less than twenty-four hours after Mouton's return, on December 9, Maryland was to play Detroit in a nonconference game the Terrapins were expected to win easily. It was a game that Mouton could sit out and it would not make a difference. He hadn't practiced in a week and there were plenty of other things on his mind. Coach Gary Williams gave Mouton the option of whether to play or not play. The decision, to Mouton, was a no-brainer.

"I really wanted to play," Mouton said. "It made me feel better to step back on the court. It's something I love to do. It kept my mind off what was going on for a while."

While basketball provided an outlet for Mouton, his teammates were wary of the situation. They knew how to be supportive, but also were careful not to cross the line and say something that might offend Mouton, who usually was one of the team's most colorful and playful characters.

"You have to act a little different," Drew Nicholas said. "Be careful what you say, not be as hard as you would be had it been a normal day. You know someone is going through something and it wouldn't be a good idea to rag on someone about basketball."

"I guess if it were a new situation for you, you wouldn't know how to handle it," Steve Blake said. "[But] the guys have been around tragedy like that. As a team, we just come closer and focus that much harder."

Because he had missed so much practice, Mouton did not start. When he entered six and a half minutes into the game, the crowd belted out the "*Moooo*" that had become a trademark whenever the boisterous Mouton did something well. He scored on Maryland's next two possessions, but the high-fives, fist pumping, and other familiar Mouton gestures were nowhere to be found on this night.

Still, Mouton was glad to be back. He finished with thirteen points, and the Terrapins won 79–54. A 91–55 victory over Monmouth ensued on December 11, and Maryland went into final exams with an eight-game winning streak.

• • •

Gary Williams is a stickler for keeping a schedule. He likes everything to be neatly organized. Practice is always at 3:45. Players had better be in uniform, ankles taped, when it is time to be on the floor. When it is time to take a bus to a game, Williams is the last one to board; when he gets on, the bus leaves.

When semester exams come around in December, though, it is Williams who has to adapt. Study and test schedules aren't as regular as class schedules. Sometimes players will be late or have to miss a practice.

And this season, as in seasons past, there was a further distraction: Cole Field House turned into a giant banquet hall for midyear graduation ceremonies, which meant that one of the nation's top college basketball teams had to practice on a court that wasn't regulation size. "It throws off your timing," Williams said of playing in a campus gym that was only about eighty-five feet long instead of the regulation ninety-four feet.

At no other time during the season does Williams worry about his team's focus the way he does in December. For some players, finals are a distraction. Others, though, see it is a necessary part of the system; they go to college to play basketball, but they have to do the classwork, too.

During finals, "basketball is still the most important thing for me," Blake said. "School is great, but I came here to play basketball. That's all I think about all the time. Basketball. It's a little distracting to have to take a little more time studying. Of course it's a little stressful. You've got to be able to handle both things. It gets tough, but it's what you have to do. It's what you're here for.

"There's some guys who probably take academics a little more seriously. But for the most part, everyone here understands that we're here to win games and play basketball. We're here to get an education, but we're here to play basketball. It's probably not the right thing to say.

"For me, basketball doesn't take a backseat to anything, really, except maybe family. Not school. I always understood school is something I have to do so I can keep playing ball. If you don't do well, you can't play. That's the attitude I've always had. As I get older, I'm starting to realize I need the education in case I don't do well playing basketball. My whole goal is to be in the NBA as a career."

It might not have been a popular opinion, but in this day and age, it was an honest one.

Regardless of whether Blake was able to practice without worrying about an English exam, Williams would have preferred to end his team's longest layoff of the season (ten days) with a few easier games to tune up for conference play. But Oklahoma had accommodated Maryland's schedule the previous season, playing in College Park in the middle of February, so the Terrapins couldn't really put up much of a fight. They would have to travel to Norman, Oklahoma, five days before Christmas.

The team's routine leading up to a road game meant taking care of media interviews at 2:45 P.M., followed by practice, a shower, and then some pizza for dinner on the bus ride to the airport. As usual, everything went like clockwork.

Most of the players arrived early, getting in some extra shooting before practice. Dixon was the last to arrive, as he almost always was, wanting to limit his interview time as much as he could. Dixon understood the obligations that came along with being a star, but he didn't always enjoy them. Rare was the day that he arrived at Cole before 3:15 for practice. But he also knew Williams's affinity for keeping a regular schedule.

"Be on time, that's rule number one," Williams said. "We'll do curfew every once in a while and we'll check it. I don't think any of our guys smoke. They know it's not good. Today, it's a little different. Less guys that play ball drink today than when I played. With what's out there financially if you can make the NBA, a lot of guys take it pretty serious to do everything they can to make the League."

When it came to alcohol, Williams said he instructed the players to avoid some local bars and not to drink. He particularly stressed the dangers and consequences of drinking and driving. Williams was speaking from experience; in May 1990, after his first season back at Maryland, he was arrested for driving while under the influence of alcohol, a charge for which he later agreed to one year of unsupervised probation.

While he might have preferred the players never to drink, he also knew that they were college students and that some enjoyed occasionally hitting College Park's nightspots.

"Guys are going to have a beer every once in a while," Williams said. "But you don't want them out before a game. The Saturday night after a game and they're off [on Sunday]? Okay, some guys are going to get out. But you really get on the driving thing. It used to be if a player got caught doing something wrong, they [the authorities] might call the coach and say something is wrong. Nowadays, they want the headlines, the celebrity catch.... And our guys are celebrities.

"But don't even think about driving. If you're out and you have two beers, people are going to say you had ten beers. The other thing is, where are all the fights when you're in college? Always around alcohol. So at the first sign of trouble, get out, you don't want to be there.... Part of the deal is you get a lot of attention and a lot of good things happen. But when anything negative is said or anything goes wrong and you're around, you will be identified."

Williams's rules were clear, and for the most part the players followed them. So on this day just before Christmas, the Terrapins adhered to his pregame schedule and boarded their charter plane on time. As they flew halfway across the country, little did most of the players know what they were in for.

Oklahoma had lost its only real test thus far, falling 67–55 at Michigan State in the Preseason NIT. And the Sooners were coming off a stretch of three games in four days, part of a schedule designed to quickly get athletic center Jabahri Brown adjusted to his new teammates. Brown, a midyear transfer from Florida International, had just become eligible, and Oklahoma coach Kelvin Sampson had wanted his new potential impact player to get in a few games before the Maryland contest, which was being hailed as a landmark game in Norman.

Now, having won seven games in a row, the Sooners were 8–1 and ranked twenty-second in the nation. They were hot and they were hungry, and the target on Maryland's back could not have been bigger. As the Terrapins pulled up to the Lloyd Noble Center for their pregame shootaround, plenty of people were milling about, eager to give Maryland a not-so-warm welcome to the nation's heartland. Clearly, this was a big game.

"The only time I saw something like that is the Kentucky people hanging around Rupp Arena for morning shooting practice," Williams said. "That probably means there's not a lot to do there. A lot of idle time.

"What our players have a hard time understanding, coming from this area with all the pro teams, [is that] in places like Norman, Oklahoma, that's the franchise. That's their Wizards or their professional franchise. Especially football at Oklahoma, but now basketball, too."

Steve Blake said he noticed the fans were particularly rowdy in the first few rows around Maryland's bench. What Blake didn't realize was that during an early television timeout, some fans stole the clipboards Maryland's student managers used to keep a running tally of stats.

At home games, Maryland might have seven or eight managers to spread out various duties, including giving out towels and water and keeping stats. On the road, though, only two or three managers are there, so during timeouts, the managers set down their clipboards and scurry about to distribute water and towels and give Gary Williams his clipboard. On this occasion, the managers left their clipboards near their seats at the end of the bench, easy prey for the unruly fans.

The managers were around the team at every practice and every game. They had seen how angry Williams could get when a player made a mistake on the court. Imagine what the red-faced coach might say or do if he found out that a manager had somehow disrupted the normal routine.

The managers "were going to cry, I thought," said Troy Wainwright, the team's director of basketball operations, who had been a team manager when he attended Maryland.

Wainwright knew the feeling. During his tenure as a manager, in a game at Duke, fans stole his stat sheets during a timeout. "At least they left my clipboard," Wainwright said. "These guys took everything."

The managers weren't the only ones to have a rough night. Maryland took an early lead, but the Terrapins never seemed to find a groove. Whether it was the long trip, the particularly noisy fans, or the unfamiliarity of the Lloyd Noble Center, Maryland made repeated mistakes. Jabahri Brown was a factor with eight points, and Oklahoma took a 36–34 lead into halftime.

The Terrapins were struggling, yes, but they felt it was their game to win. They had played poorly in the first half, with ten turnovers, yet still hung around with the athletic, talented Sooners. That would change in the second half, though not the way Williams had hoped.

Lonny Baxter and Juan Dixon scored on Maryland's first two possessions, but the seniors would not score another point. A steal and layup by Byron Mouton brought the Terrapins within three, 52–49, with seven minutes left. After that, however, Maryland would not get another field goal until the closing minutes. To the crowd's delight, the Sooners scored ten consecutive points en route to a 72–56 victory.

Dixon missed all four of his three-point attempts and finished with eleven points, one of his lowest totals of the season. Baxter nearly had a triple-double, with nine points, ten rebounds, and six turnovers. Maryland had been outrebounded twenty-six to fourteen in the second half.

"They kind of just put it to us physically and athletically," Blake said. "Just one of those games where you're not playing well and we weren't reacting well to what they were doing. Sometimes, when it goes wrong, it goes wrong and there is nothing you can do about it.

"We don't get blown out like that very often. Ever. To have that happen, it's like, 'When is this going to be over so we can finally get out of it?' "

Even when the final buzzer sounded, Maryland's trip was far from over. In the visiting locker room, Gary Williams was livid at his players, getting angrier than he would at any other time during the course of the season.

"He was furious, to say the least," Drew Nicholas said, "because he was kind of looking at it as all we had to do was come out and win that game and take a few days off before Christmas. But things didn't work out like that."

Normally, Williams is brief in his postgame remarks, trying to be positive and look ahead to the next game. On this night, though, he took several extra minutes to deliver a message.

"I just didn't want them to use finals and all that stuff as an excuse for not playing well," Williams said. "There could be a snowstorm where you have trouble getting to the place"—such as two seasons before, when a game at North Carolina was delayed by one day—"but you never want to use that as an excuse for not playing well.

"I thought they pushed us around. The refs were letting both teams play physical. It was a physical game. We didn't take advantage of it. You shouldn't get pushed around.

"I don't know if it was conditioning or what, but in the second half, they were too quick for us, too physical for us, and they got us. The good thing about the team was that after the Arizona game and after that game, you couldn't shake the confidence of our team. That was on national TV, that was a bad loss, and there were a lot of things bad about that, but it wasn't like we thought we were in a lot of trouble. That's where you have a veteran team. The year before, when Duke beat us, we probably didn't have that same confidence in ourselves. But having gone through that and having gone to the Final Four, after that we had a certain toughness about us. We knew how to come back from a tough loss."

The plane ride home was especially quiet. Williams wanted this loss to hurt more than usual. A few players talked in hushed tones about what went wrong, but there was little noise.

• • •

It was about 3 A.M. on Saturday, December 22, when the team got back to campus. Nobody was in the mood to do much of anything, and College Park had pretty much cleared out, with the rest of the student body home for semester break.

Had Maryland played well and won, Williams might have given his players off until Christmas night, when the team would gather for practice before its December 27 game against William & Mary.

After their forgetful performance in Norman, though, Williams was not nearly as forgiving. He wanted to make sure his players understood exactly where their coach was coming from and how angry he was about the Oklahoma debacle.

There were practices on Saturday and Sunday, before Williams dismissed the players for the holiday. Williams caught a flight to Columbus,

Ohio, on Christmas Eve to deliver a few presents to Kristin, her husband, Geoff, and Williams's grandson, David. The coach was in Ohio less than twenty-four hours. "Spoil my grandson and move on," said Williams. "A couple trucks. A check for my daughter and son-in-law. Maryland clothes for my grandson.

"One problem with coaching is that Thanksgiving, Christmas, and New Year's are the three biggest holidays for a lot of people. But as a coach, there is a lot of stress around them. You worry about players getting out of a normal routine because you're out of school. And as a coach, you're always worried about your next game. Always. Especially at that time of year, because you haven't proven you're a good basketball team."

Having played Santa Claus, Williams was back at Maryland on Christmas Day for practice.

The holidays are a difficult time for the players. They miss, or catch only part of, family get-togethers. Back on campus, few classmates are around. The only thing that worked to Williams's advantage this season was that his players were veterans; of those who received any meaningful playing time, only Ryan Randle had not been through this. The others, while they didn't like it, were accustomed to the schedule and to playing before the quieter, calmer crowds that attended games when most of the students were away.

Two days later, Maryland started slowly against William & Mary but used a 15–0 run bridging halftime to take control. The final score was 103–75. The Terrapins were 9–2, and their Atlantic Coast Conference opener was next, December 30 at North Carolina State.

• • •

Before Maryland made the trip to Raleigh, some tactical changes were in order. The Terrapins were playing well enough to clobber overmatched foes, but they weren't reaching their potential.

Blake and Dixon were established in the backcourt. Mouton was the team's only true small forward. Baxter was a force inside. At power forward, though, the Terrapins had options. Tahj Holden had replaced Chris Wilcox in the starting lineup after the season opener, but Holden never seemed to get going, perhaps because of the knee he had hyperextended in the preseason.

"That's the problem I've had pretty much my whole career," Holden said. "I get hurt and I wouldn't be consistent, wouldn't be aggressive.... It was real frustrating, very frustrating. The only thing you can do to correct it is go out and play hard, practice hard. You can't think about it, you can't focus on it."

Holden hadn't played poorly, but he hadn't exceeded expectations, either. When the conference schedule began, Wilcox would be back in the starting lineup. He had scored a team-high fifteen points in the loss at Oklahoma and eleven points against William & Mary, and his energy seemed to give the team a boost. Plus, Williams sensed that Wilcox was better prepared if he knew when he was going into the game.

"Chris just seemed to play better when he started," Williams said. "All guys at this level have started all their lives. Some guys can adjust to not starting; some can't."

CHAPTER 7

A Heavyweight Title Fight

With one look around the table, Gary Williams could see just how things had changed since he was hired to return to Maryland in 1989.

When Williams joined the ACC, Mike Krzyzewski, the short guy with the long name, was just getting things rolling at Duke. Bobby Cremins, with his trademark white hair and ability to say just about anything, was becoming an institution at Georgia Tech. Dean Smith was ruling the roost from Chapel Hill. Jim Valvano had won a national championship at North Carolina State. Terry Holland was quite successful at Virginia. Dave Odom was at Wake Forest, Cliff Ellis at Clemson.

Fast-forward to the fall of 2001, when Williams could look around the table at the ACC's annual preseason meeting of coaches and see only one face that had been there longer than his. It was another reminder that coaches have short life spans—when you're winning, you're gold, but when you're losing, a new coach is only a phone call and a few dollars away.

Holland was now the athletic director at Virginia, which had canned his successor, Jeff Jones, and hired fast-talking Pete Gillen.

State's Valvano had passed away from cancer, and his replacement, Les Robinson, had himself been replaced, by slow-talking Herb Sendek.

El Deano had retired and passed the reins to the grandfatherly Bill Guthridge, who later retired, to be replaced by the energetic Matt Doherty, another coach from the North Carolina family.

Cremins, his charm wearing thin without an NCAA tournament appearance in four seasons, had resigned, and Paul Hewitt had brought his fast-paced style to Georgia Tech.

Cliff Ellis had been replaced by Rick Barnes, who then went on to Texas; Larry Shyatt was now the head coach at Clemson.

Odom had left Wake Forest the previous spring for South Carolina, and Skip Prosser was now in charge of the Demon Deacons.

Steve Robinson was another new face; his Florida State team was still an independent when Williams was hired as Maryland's head coach and didn't join the ACC until two years after Williams's arrival.

Of the league's nine coaches, only Duke's Krzyzewski had more tenure than Williams; he was entering his twenty-second season at the fine private school in Durham, North Carolina. And since Krzyzewski was born on February 13, 1947, it was Williams who held the title as the ACC's oldest coach.

"I've been here a while now," Williams said. "I never thought I'd be the oldest coach in the conference."

Williams had always enjoyed being one of the guys, but now he had few contemporaries. With the conference holding its annual preseason media day at the Grandover Resort in Greensboro, North Carolina, there was no one in particular that Williams wanted to sit next to during the coaches' meeting.

"When I started, there were definitely personalities," Williams said, chuckling as he remembered how he had enjoyed the company of Dean

Smith, watching Smith chew his nicotine gum after he had stopped smoking. "There's a tendency nowadays, the politically correct thing, not to show your true feelings. Sometimes back then, when I started, it was no holds barred. You said whatever was on your mind. It was a lot of funny stuff. Nowadays, the meetings are a lot more cut-and-dry.

"Things change. You're not as close [to other coaches]. There's an age difference now."

Older, yes. Less competitive? No way.

Maryland had come through the majority of its nonconference schedule in fine shape, with a record of 9–2. Seniors Juan Dixon and Lonny Baxter were playing like leaders, and the Terrapins seemed right on course to challenge rival Duke for the ACC championship.

The first step would come with the game at North Carolina State, the first of Maryland's three trips to the Research Triangle region. By the time the season was over, the players would know the service roads in and around Raleigh-Durham International Airport as if they were in College Park.

Although State had finished with a losing record in conference play for the past ten seasons, there was hope in Wolfpack country. State had a veteran backcourt in Archie Miller and Anthony Grundy and a promising group of freshmen that included 6-foot-6-inch Julius Hodge, one of the most talented players to come out of New York City in quite some time.

For all his talent, Hodge already had acquired, less than two months into the season, a reputation for running his mouth and pulling knucklehead stunts, drawing the ire of upperclassmen. Before tip-off, Maryland's players heard Hodge talking smack in the direction of Juan Dixon.

"Some guys may be able to talk," Maryland guard Drew Nicholas said. "But not a freshman coming in all arrogant in his first ACC game. You don't want to hear that. He had no clue what the ACC was like."

The talking went on all game. And so did the fouls. In all, there would be fifty-seven fouls, eighty-one free throws, and thirty-two turnovers in a game that lasted nearly two and a half hours—25 percent longer than a typical game.

Maryland led by as many as ten points in the first half but couldn't put the game away. State rallied, and when Marcus Melvin made a three-pointer from the right wing midway through the second half to give the Wolfpack its first lead, 44–43, an upset was in sight.

Maryland clearly was frustrated—with its own offensive struggles, with the Wolfpack's physical defense, and with Hodge, who, the Terrapins said, rarely stopped talking.

The game stayed close until the final minutes, when point guard Steve Blake made perhaps his biggest shots of the season to that point. Known more for his passing, Blake came off a pick by Lonny Baxter and made a short jumper from the right side for his first basket of the game, giving Maryland a 57–52 lead. Melvin made two free throws for State, and then Blake drained a three-pointer from the left side. It was 60–54 with 1:42 left, the Terrapins' biggest lead since the first half. Blake and Dixon made all ten of their free-throw attempts in the final minute, and Maryland held on, 72–65, to make Williams the tenth coach to win one hundred ACC games. Chris Wilcox, back in the starting lineup, had nine points and twelve rebounds.

It hadn't been pretty, but nobody wearing Maryland red really cared. Winning on the road was what good teams did. Doing it when the team hadn't played well made the victory even sweeter.

Generally undetected at the time was the fact that midway through the second half, Blake had slapped Hodge in the stomach, sending Hodge crumpling to the floor. No foul was called and nothing was said, but it was a play that would make news a month later.

Four days after the N.C. State game, with center Lonny Baxter resting a sprained ankle he had suffered in practice, Maryland opened 2002 with a 92–65 pelting of Norfolk State, its eighty-fourth consecutive victory in a nonconference home game, the longest streak in the nation. The Terrapins' only nonconference home loss under Williams came on December 12, 1989, to Coppin State.

Maryland had bounced back from its loss at Oklahoma with three consecutive victories. Two had been gimmes, but the win at N.C. State had provided a shot of confidence.

• • •

Next up was North Carolina, a team that had provided the Terrapins plenty of heartbreak over the years. This season's version of the Tar Heels, though, was reeling. After playing in twenty-seven consecutive NCAA tournaments and winning at least twenty games in thirty-one consecutive seasons, this team looked more like a squad from one of UNC's satellite campuses—although that might be an insult to the folks in Greensboro and Asheville, among others.

North Carolina had started the season with losses to Hampton, Davidson, and Indiana, going 0–3 for the first time since 1928—three years before a certain Kansan named Dean Smith was born. The Tar Heels came to College Park off an 84–62 shellacking at twenty-third-ranked Wake Forest, but that game was nothing compared with the beating Maryland gave the Heels on January 9.

Juan Dixon, growing his hair out to try to win a bet with teammates, scored fourteen of his game-high twenty-nine points in the opening six minutes. The game was never close. Maryland's 112–79 victory was the most lopsided ever in the series, and the Terrapins' tally represented the most points ever allowed by North Carolina.

"Yeah, they scored 112 points," North Carolina forward Jason Capel said. "They hit threes. They got dunks. They got alley-oops. They put on a show. They beat the hell out of us."

Baxter returned from his ankle injury and finished with nine points and seven rebounds in twenty-four minutes. And his backup, junior college transfer Ryan Randle, had nine points in twelve minutes, his second strong game in a row; with Baxter out against Norfolk State, Randle had had twelve points, eight rebounds, and five blocks. Earlier in the season, it was obvious that Coach Gary Williams had not trusted Randle. Off these performances, though, perhaps it was time to give Sleepy a chance.

With the game out of hand from the opening minutes, perhaps the most interesting part of the night was how the coaches dealt with such a one-sided game. North Carolina's Matt Doherty stomped his foot, berated official Karl Hess, and was called for a technical foul after Dixon got away with an apparent walk on a breakaway layup, the kind of violation that almost never is called.

Later in the first half, an angry Gary Williams called a timeout after consecutive three-pointers by Carolina had narrowed the lead to a slim 43–26. Williams, who had been calm earlier, was ranting and waving his arms, his once-perfect gray hair scattered in all directions. Perhaps the timeout was valid, though; the Tar Heels actually were shooting better than 50 percent, but their turnovers never gave them a chance.

A few minutes later, after Maryland allowed a dunk and another three-pointer to make it a 51–37 game, Williams called another timeout. It had to be the first time ever that a Maryland coach was not satisfied with a fourteen-point lead over North Carolina. The message got across. Williams didn't want his team to take anyone lightly, regardless of the situation. Almighty Duke three days earlier had been beaten by lowly Florida State. If the Seminoles could beat Duke, Maryland could lose to anyone left on its schedule. Playing like this in the postseason would prompt another round of speculation about whether the Terrapins could put away inferior teams.

By halftime, it was 57–37. The only suspense in the final twenty minutes was whether this game would overtake North Carolina's forty-three-point loss to the Lynchburg Elks in 1915 as the worst loss in school history. Otherwise, television viewers were left to wonder whether announcer Dick Vitale actually would run out of things to talk about.

The postgame was much more interesting than anything that had happened on the court. With reporters wondering how it felt to beat a traditional power so badly, Steve Blake blurted out, "Who's Carolina? It's just another team."

Blake later explained that he had meant no malice and that reporters were making too much out of the lopsided score. "Someone asked me the question the same time over and over, 'Can you believe that it was Carolina you did this to?'" Blake said. "Eventually, I was like, 'You act like they're a god or something.' I think it was out of context a little bit. I was basically directing it to him that it's just another team, that's how I look at it."

It was Maryland's eleventh consecutive victory in Cole, and with the Terrapins back on a roll, all that stood in the way of next week's showdown at Duke was a game at Georgia Tech.

• • •

The folks at Georgia Tech might want to call the ACC office and thank them for nothing. The Yellow Jackets had the privilege of traveling to Durham to play top-ranked Duke after the Blue Devils' first loss of the season, then returning to Atlanta to play fourth-ranked Maryland.

Georgia Tech's trip to Duke had been nothing short of a nightmare. After the loss at Florida State, Duke coach Mike Krzyzewski had decided to make things "tough" on his players. The chairs and the engraved nameplates and pictures above each player's stall were removed from the locker room, with the intent of making a point that such amenities needed to be earned. Also, somehow, guard Chris Duhon had the notion that other teams thought the Blue Devils had become patsies.

"Everybody has been disrespecting us," Duhon told reporters after a 104–79 victory over Georgia Tech. "Everyone has been calling us soft and everyone's been saying we're not tough, and that's never happened to a Duke team."

No one was quite sure who disrespected Duke or thought its players soft, although some Blue Devils said Georgia Tech did not act properly when it took up more than half the court for some pregame stretching. Georgia Tech coach Paul Hewitt said that perhaps the Blue Devils needed to "contrive some things to get themselves motivated" and pledged to remind his players to stay on their side of the court when touching their toes.

Similarly, many in attendance and watching on television were perplexed by the behavior of Krzyzewski. With the Blue Devils leading 28–8, he drew a technical foul after Duke center Carlos Boozer was assessed an intentional foul. As Georgia Tech's players shot the ensuing free throws, Krzyzewski turned to the crowd and wildly waved his arms, inciting the fans. The postgame handshake between coaches also was bizarre, as Krzyzewski sharply thrust out his right hand toward Hewitt and his assistants.

Although Krzyzewski never explained his emotional outbursts, television analyst Dan Bonner said he believed the coach was trying to transfer his intensity to the players.

"Mike is a little intense about this particular team. That's my impression, [although] I have not talked with Mike about this," Bonner said a few days later. "I have the impression the Duke coaching staff feels like this is a team they really have to drive and they have to be incredibly intense with. And through their intensity, they can drive the team's intensity."

After being trounced by Duke, Georgia Tech appeared in trouble against Maryland, falling behind 48–33 late in the first half. The Terrapins had lost in their previous two trips to Alexander Memorial Coliseum, but seemed well on their way to victory until a ragged start to the second half. With two and a half minutes left, Maryland's lead was a tenuous 81–79. It was 85–83 when Baxter underthrew a lob pass to Wilcox and Georgia Tech made the steal, giving the Yellow Jackets a chance to tie the game.

As Terrapin killer Tony Akins brought the ball up the court, however, Juan Dixon was ready to make yet another highlight. Dixon stayed in Akins's blind spot, hoping that the left-handed Akins would switch his dribble from his right hand to his left.

And when it happened, Dixon pounced, like a cat after prey. With his right hand, he deftly stole the ball, then immediately headed in the other direction. Still forty feet from the basket, Dixon saw Wilcox sticking a finger in the air, pleading for a lob pass. For most, it was a risky play. The easy thing to do was hold the ball and wait for Georgia Tech to foul; Dixon, a 90 percent free-throw shooter on the season, certainly could take care of things from the line.

Dixon, though, never lacked confidence. Neither did Wilcox, who seemed to have springs in his shoes. Dixon threw the pass, Wilcox stuffed it home over Robert Brooks (who somehow was not called for a foul despite significant contact), and the game essentially was over. Maryland had improved to 13–2 with a 92–87 victory.

"I don't say a lot of pretty things about my players or blow smoke about them, but . . . that steal he had on the sideline was an incredible play," Gary Williams said. "It seems like he makes [plays] at the right time. A lot of guys make great plays—his happen in that situation.

"For what he has done for Maryland, I don't think there is any other player who has had a greater impact for his team."

With the college basketball season heating up, the steal and alley-oop dunk were on all of the highlight shows. Juan Dixon, everyone knew. Chris Wilcox, though, had been in the shadows on a veteran team. Now, with each powerful dunk, he was moving toward the spotlight.

• • •

Like it or not, the Maryland Terrapins knew they were judged on how they measured up to Duke. The fierce nature of the rivalry initially surprised Byron Mouton, who had grown up in Louisiana. "Duke, Duke, Duke," Mouton once said. "That's all I ever hear about is Duke."

Now in his third year at Maryland, Mouton had a full grasp of what had grown into the nation's hottest rivalry.

"I got brainwashed into all this 'We've got to beat Duke.' It's crazy how fascinated people are," he said. "No matter what is going on, they want us to beat Duke. They don't even talk about the national championship, they talk about beating Duke. 'I hate Duke.' That's all they say."

Some of the stories Mouton would relay to his mother in Louisiana. The alumni who would approach Mouton after games and tell him that they were looking forward to a special victory over the hated Blue Devils. The students around campus and in class who would convey their feelings. It all rubbed off. "When I played, I wanted to kill them," Mouton said. "The fans are so into it. They just brainwash you into it. You want to do it for the fans."

There was also some jealousy on the part of Maryland's players, who felt they still were considered backup singers to the headlining Blue Devils. "Most of the players on our team see Duke always getting accolades, All-Americans, preseason number one. Their biggest fan is Dick Vitale," Mouton said.

For years, the series had been one-sided. Duke had won twenty-nine of the teams' previous thirty-four meetings before Juan Dixon led Maryland to victory in Durham on February 9, 2000, the game that prompted students back in College Park to tear down the Byrd Stadium goalposts. The next season, on senior night for Duke superstar Shane Battier, Dixon again led the Terrapins to victory, the first time in eighteen years that Maryland had won on consecutive trips to cozy Cameron Indoor Stadium. Although Duke won three of the team's four meetings in the 2000–01 season, every game was emotional and close, and there was no mistaking the deep feelings that went into each game.

"The game has gotten big," Gary Williams said. "At first, it wasn't big for Duke. We had to get better before it became a rivalry. It took a while. Now it's a national perception that it's really a great game every year. We'll see if that continues. Let's face it: Duke has been as good a program as there has been in the country the last fifteen years. So naturally, if we can challenge them, that's going to be a good rivalry."

Although Duke had won sixty-seven of its previous seventy-one home games, Maryland's players relished the trip to Durham. If you took an informal poll of the Terrapins, it might have been unanimous: of the eight other arenas in the ACC, Cameron was their favorite place to play. For starters, the players loved the challenge of going into a noisy building and trying to quiet the annoying crowd. At Duke, that included the guy about twenty rows behind the visiting bench who twirled a white towel like a lasso, prompting the students to chant *"Crazy Towel Guy"* whenever he went into his act. And on the court, no place had rims as soft as Cameron's or so little room behind the baskets; these factors created excellent sight lines—perhaps one of the reasons the Blue Devils always shot their three-pointers so well.

Sports Illustrated rated Cameron the fourth-best sporting venue of the twentieth century, behind only Yankee Stadium, Augusta National Golf Club, and West Point's Michie Stadium.

"I actually like playing in their gym," Steve Blake said, before alluding to the cheat sheets of cheers that are distributed before each game at Cameron. "It's a lot of fun. I believe the toughest place to play in the ACC, other than Maryland, is Virginia. The Duke fans are just so much more organized that on TV, it looks like they're just amazing."

Said Williams, "You know they're always good and going to play hard. It's a challenge to win there. Not many teams win there."

Duke entered the game 14–1, 3–1 in the ACC, and ranked number one in the country. Maryland was 13–2, at 3–0 the only team unbeaten in the conference, and number three in the nation. It was only January 17, but there was plenty at stake. For starters, Maryland's players felt that in order to be successful, they had to be able to beat Duke, the team that had kept them from winning the ACC and NCAA titles the previous season. Also, win this game, the Terrapins felt, and they might ascend to the number-one spot in the polls for the first time in school history.

The game started at a breakneck pace, both teams scoring almost at will. There were twenty-six lead changes and three ties in the first half. Duke guard Jason Williams was unstoppable. In games past, Blake had been able to match up one-on-one against Williams and contain the high-scoring guard, but Blake was now playing closer to Williams, trying to alter his shots. The result was that Williams often drove past Blake, either finishing or passing to a teammate for an easy shot as Maryland's other defenders tried to give help. Soon Maryland switched Dixon onto Williams.

A quick seven-point spurt on a Williams layup, a steal and dunk by Duhon, and a three-pointer by Daniel Ewing—all in less than forty seconds—gave Duke a 29–22 lead. Maryland hounded the offensive boards and retook the lead on a jump hook by Wilcox, who again was playing well in a big game. Duke led 37–36 when Krzyzewski, who rarely went deep into his bench, inserted seldom-used guard Andre Buckner for Jason Williams. Gary Williams, for some reason wanting to match Krzyzewski's move, countered by putting in his little-used point guard, Andre Collins, for Dixon.

It was almost comical. Here were two of the nation's top three teams, and for some reason, late in the first half, guys who often never took off their warm-ups were in one of the season's biggest games. The stars returned about forty seconds later, but it was another backup, center Ryan Randle, who gave Maryland a boost while Baxter sat out with two fouls.

Tahj Holden passed out of a double team to Randle for a three-point play; then Randle followed his own miss, and later Dixon penetrated and passed to Randle for a layup. Randle hadn't even played at Oklahoma and had been in for only one minute against N.C. State. Now, in an extremely important situation, he had scored the Terrapins' final seven points of the half, and Maryland led 49–48.

"That was a great first half," Gary Williams said. "Both teams were trying to play defense. It didn't matter. Guys were shooting the ball too well."

As the teams took the floor for the second half, Duke forward Dahntay Jones slapped the floor with both palms and stared at Dixon, whom he would guard. Dixon quickly shot back, "You're going down. Watch."

The half started just as the first one had ended, with the teams combining to make ten of their first twelve shots. Duke took a 58–57 lead when Jason Williams blew past Dixon for a driving layup. Then Williams forced his way into the lane and banked in a shot. Baxter was called for a charge and Maryland called timeout, hoping to stop the Blue Devils' momentum. Fifteen seconds later, though, Williams nailed a three-pointer from the left wing and it was 63–57.

Maryland got close only once, when Drew Nicholas's short jumper from the right side made it 73–70. That prompted Krzyzewski to call timeout, and soon Duke regained its big lead. Forward Mike Dunleavy made a bank shot and a fast-break three-pointer, and Williams followed with a steal and dunk. The Cameron Crazies were going nuts: "*J-Will, J-Will rock you!*" they chanted.

Maryland did not make a field goal in the final 7:55, and Dixon finished with a season-low ten points. The final was 99–78, as Jason Williams finished with thirty-four points, eight assists, and seven rebounds.

"We just didn't have the same energy in the second half," Gary Williams said. "I'm not talking about a big change, but a small percentage difference against Duke can change the game."

Perhaps the one time Duke slowed down was after the game, when Krzyzewski took longer than usual to get to the postgame interview room, which was located about fifteen feet from the Blue Devils' stripped-down locker room.

After any game, and especially after a loss, all the visiting team wants to do is leave. For the Terrapins, there was a bus trip, a plane ride, and another bus trip ahead before they would get back to Cole Field House in the middle of the night. Gary Williams rarely takes long to deliver his postgame speech to the team, and this night was no different. The problem was that, at Duke, both coaches conduct their postgame news conferences in the same room, and barring extraordinary circumstances, Krzyzewski always goes first.

Once Williams had finished speaking to the players, Maryland's locker room was opened to the media, and Williams thought it would be a only few minutes before he could walk up the stairs to court level, then walk diagonally across the court to the interview room. But even after Maryland's locker room had been open for several minutes, Krzyzewski still hadn't arrived for what surely would be a long session with the media after such a big victory.

"Who the hell does he think he is?" Williams roared, dispatching the team's publicist to tell the media that the Maryland coach would not attend the news conference, although he later relented. "He's just another coach."

• • •

Winter break is a great time for college basketball teams. True, campuses are mostly empty while the general student body enjoys time off, but coaches like the fact that their teams can practice as often as they want, whenever they want, and the players have few other concerns. Unlike when school is in session, the NCAA does not require players to have at least one day off per week.

Since the Terrapins did not get back to campus until early Friday morning after the Duke loss Thursday night, Gary Williams did not want to put his team through a grueling workout with Clemson coming to town on Sunday. The coach did, however, want to spend time with his players and impress upon them the need to work harder.

"The good thing in a game like that is that win or lose, you know you have to play better defense," Williams said. "The day after that game, you walk into practice and say, 'We have to play a little better defense that that,' and you're not going to get any disagreement from them.

"You can't play defense like that. We had to get a little smarter defensively. I think we became a better team defensively as the year went on. Wilcox started to see where he could be more of a factor. Not just blocking shots, but intimidating people. Juan was playing such that other guys started to pick up off Juan's ability to anticipate passes. We became a very good rebounding team. That's a big part of defense, if you can hold a team to one shot. We had a lot of pride, we didn't like giving up open shots."

Measuring defense was tough to do. Success might be something as simple as forcing an opponent to take a twenty-foot jump shot instead of a fifteen-footer. On occasion, Williams might be able to tell when an opponent was uncomfortable running its offense.

Measuring his team's heartbeat was a little easier for Williams. While last season's first loss to Duke had started a midseason swoon, the coach sensed no such repeat. In the 2001 game, Maryland had blown a ten-point lead in the final minute of regulation, a devastating defeat. This past game, though, was different. After this loss, unlike the gone-in-fifty-four-seconds debacle of 2001, Maryland's players and coaches did not feel crushed. The path to the national championship, they felt, still went through Duke, but the Terrapins pointed to one of the most amazing first halves of the season and said that if they could play at that level all the time, they were in the hunt. The Terrapins simply had been unable to keep pace and had been beaten by a very good team. In the locker room, nobody felt that Maryland had lost because it was not as good as Duke.

"It's disappointing," Blake said, "because we were in the game and just that quickly, we blew it on our own."

"We've just got to bounce back," Dixon said. "We can't afford to go in a slump like we did last year, and I don't think we will."

Williams said he planned no drastic changes and, like his team, gave the appearance of remaining remarkably upbeat. In reference to Duke, he cracked, "We still have our pictures in our locker room."

• • •

January 20, a Sunday, provided what would be a rare snowfall in the Washington area. While it was cold and snowy outside, though, it again was hot inside Cole Field House, in the stands and on the court. Both teams started quickly, Maryland pounding the ball inside to Baxter and Wilcox, Clemson raining in three-pointers, including ten of its first thirteen tries.

Maryland had a 52–48 lead at halftime, but it was unable to pull away in the second half. The Tigers rallied, and back-to-back three-pointers by Edward Scott and Tony Stockman gave Clemson an 80–78 lead with six minutes left. The Terrapins, though, had plenty of answers. Dixon and Blake made three-pointers, and Maryland led 93–88 with ninety seconds left when Dixon delivered another clutch play.

With the shot clock running down, Dixon posted up Dwon Clifton on the right side of the lane and made a fadeaway shot while being fouled. Dixon's free throw made it 96–88, and victory was secure. The final score was 99–90. It wasn't aesthetically pleasing by any stretch, but no one was going to complain. Dixon and Baxter had twenty-three and twenty-one points, respectively, and Wilcox added seventeen points and fourteen rebounds.

"It's all about winning," said Dixon, who broke Johnny Rhodes's school record for three-point shots in a career. "It doesn't matter how you get it, whether it is ugly or looks good."

The Terrapins followed Clemson with an impressive performance, winning 85–63 at number-twenty-one Wake Forest. Maryland's lead had been 40–32 early in the second half when Wake Forest's Josh Howard was called for a technical foul after backhanding Mouton in the face, continuing what was a budding rivalry between the players.

"I had a real bad hip pointer and I think he knew," Howard said. "He kept hitting it and hitting it until finally one time that was it.

"He's like any other player, trying to help his teammates out. A couple other teams probably think I'm a dirty player."

It was just the latest in a series of skirmishes involving Mouton. At the previous season's ACC tournament, according to Mouton and other Maryland players, North Carolina State's Clifford Crawford got in Mouton's face and threatened him as the teams passed each other. Crawford said the incident was less confrontational. Also that season, according to those familiar with what took place, Howard accused Mouton of grabbing more than a handful below the belt as Howard tried to drive the lane.

"Whoever I'm guarding, I want to make them mad," Mouton said. "Unless I know you, then I'm going to leave you alone. Coach always tries to put me on the best perimeter player. My main thing was to get that person so mad, so aggravated. That was my goal.

"Most opponents hate me. A lot of people love me, too. There is no in-between."

Before Maryland's January 26 game against visiting Florida State, Gary Williams wrote one word on a dry-erase board in the locker room: REVENGE.

Duke's miracle comeback the previous season may have sent Maryland into a tailspin, but it was Florida State that had delivered a potentially crushing blow. On Valentine's Day, the Seminoles had shocked the Terrapins, 74–71. Maryland's players remembered seeing Florida State guard Delvon Arrington leap onto the scorer's table with his arms raised and how the Terrapins were booed off their own court. Williams remembered that one fan yelled at him, "Have fun in the NIT."

That night, Dixon sat alone in the half-lit weight room for more than an hour after the game, wearing only a pair of shorts and staring into a wall of mirrors. He felt guilty, somehow blaming himself for the loss and the team's downward spiral, and wanted to be by himself. As he looked into the mirrors, Dixon promised to himself that he would turn things around. He began lifting weights and practicing his shot more often, even staying late into the night. While classmates were partying, Dixon was in the gym until 1:30 A.M. some nights.

With Dixon leading the way, Maryland had turned things around and gone to the Final Four. Now, with another chance at Florida State, Dixon turned in one of his finest performances, with twenty-five points, eleven rebounds, and eight steals, leading the Terrapins to an 84–63 victory.

"What I like about Juan the most is when there are plays to be made, he wants to take the shot," Williams said. "There are some plays that count more than two points. He seems to come up with the plays to change a game."

Beating Florida State set up another chance to make amends, with a trip to Virginia up next, on January 31.

Maryland had lost on its past two visits to Charlottesville, getting creamed 99–78 in 2001 and falling in overtime, 89–87, in the 2000 regular season finale.

University Hall was a strange place to play. Even though it was the ACC's smallest arena, there were almost always empty seats for games, regardless of the opponent. Students rarely used all of their ticket allotment, but they could be noisy and grated on opposing teams. According to an *ESPN The Magazine* story, some fans taunted Dixon by chanting "*Crackhead parents*" before the game, nearly inciting an irate Dixon to take on the crowd. And perhaps the students' favorite chant was directed at Blake. "*Little Steevee, Little Steevee,*" they loved to serenade.

"We just never play well when we go down there," Blake said. "Their fans are crazy, too. They really get on you hard. For some reason, I don't know what it is, when we go down there, we don't play [well]. The fans are loud. They're right there on the court. And the fans are obnoxious.... The Cameron Crazies, they're organized. But Virginia fans are a little wacko in the head. I like it when people are like that.... Our fans are the worst. But they're just a little further back."

Needing a win to keep pace with Duke in the ACC standings, Maryland seemed to be in trouble in the second half. Virginia's Travis Watson converted a fast-break three-point play; then Chris Williams blocked a shot, and Keith Jenifer, a Baltimore native who had not been offered a scholarship by Maryland, made an open fifteen-footer from the right wing. With 6:19 left, Virginia had taken a 74–70 lead, and another long, quiet bus ride up Route 29 back to College Park seemed to be in the forecast.

"Man, here we go again," Blake thought to himself.

Then came perhaps the season's defining stretch. As Maryland brought the ball into the frontcourt, Gary Williams called a timeout. Mouton, standing in front of the Terrapins' bench and as usual in the middle of things, had the ball clasped between his hands, with his elbows to the side to protect the ball as Watson tried to get it. After the whistle blew for the timeout, Mouton raised his elbows, grazing Watson, who didn't seem to mind. Jenifer, though, was in the vicinity, and as the Terrapins tried to huddle, Jenifer was in no hurry to leave.

Gary Williams was about to blow a gasket. Not only was his team on verge of being blown out—again—but he felt an opposing player, a freshman, was showing up the Terrapins. Williams afterward didn't want to talk about specifics, but there was no mistaking the words that raced from his lips. "Get the fuck out of here!" the television cameras caught Williams screaming.

"Your huddle is your huddle," Williams explained later. "You don't want other people in your huddle."

Before Williams had finished yelling, though, Virginia assistant coach Walt Fuller, who looks more like a football lineman, came charging down the sideline from the home-team bench. Official Duke Edsall intercepted Fuller, preventing a full-scale donnybrook. Virginia coach Pete Gillen, perhaps the only coach in the ACC who might win a sweat-off against Williams, met near midcourt with Williams and game officials to discuss what had just occurred and try to ease the tension. But by the time the teams took the court, with the crowd growing louder by the second, it had all the feel of a heavyweight title fight.

Jenifer "was trying to show everybody that he was tough," Mouton said. "It was funny, because our whole coaching staff got into it. Nobody was backing down from nobody. Coach always says we're a team and we're going to fight together. From that moment on, everybody was into it. When we see our whole coaching staff fighting, they're fighting for us and we've got to fight for them."

Things would get worse before they got better for Maryland. Virginia's Roger Mason made two free throws, then drained an open three-pointer from the right corner. Blake, having an off night with just four assists and three turnovers, threw the ball away, leading to a tip-in by Watson. After Dixon missed a jumper, Watson scored while being fouled. It was 83–74 with 3:22 left, and Gary Williams's biggest concern was that his team not lose by twenty.

Before Watson missed his ensuing free throw, Williams substituted Drew Nicholas for the erratic Blake and Ryan Randle for Baxter. It was an odd switch, taking out the starting point guard and starting center, but it worked. Dixon made two free throws, and then Wilcox stole a pass near midcourt and went in for a high-flying dunk.

Virginia called a timeout and briefly stemmed the tide when Chris Williams drove for a basket, but he missed a subsequent free throw. Still, it was 85–78 with 2:40 left.

With Maryland trailing by such a large margin with little time left, Nicholas wasn't hesitant about shooting. If he missed, so what? But he didn't. First he made a long three-pointer from the right wing. Later, after two free throws by Mouton, Nicholas coolly hit a twenty-five-footer from well beyond the top of the key. Maryland trailed 87–86 with 1:21 left, but the Terrapins could smell victory. Baxter, back in the game, somehow blocked Watson from behind without committing a foul, and then Dixon floated in a running shot from along the left baseline. Maryland had the lead, 88–87, with 31.8 seconds left. Virginia missed, Tahj Holden made two free throws, and then Nicholas blocked a last-second three-point shot by Mason.

Maryland had done the unthinkable, rallying for a 91–87 victory. It was only January 31, but this was the kind of win that would have long-term ramifications. It also was a breakthrough night for Nicholas, whom Coach Williams called "Drew Nickels." He had scored only six points, but his ability to stand up and deliver when it looked as if the game was lost had shown the coaches something.

"My mentality was, 'If I get a shot, I'm shooting it. If I get a three, I'm shooting it. What else are we going to lose right now? If Coach is going to take me out for taking a bad shot, so be it,'" Nicholas said.

While Nicholas basked in the moment, one of his closest friends, Blake, was struggling with his emotions. Blake was ecstatic that the team had pulled out a victory, but on an individual level he was less than pleased.

"I was disappointed that I wasn't playing well and I wasn't helping the team," Blake said. "At the same time, once I saw Drew doing so well, I'm part of the team, I've got to be happy and root for the team. I had to take on a different role. It was tough. I'm always used to being out there at the end of the game. I was thinking to myself, 'If I'm a real team player, I should be happy that Drew is playing well and getting us back into the game and not mad that I'm not in the game.'"

Whatever Blake was feeling, Maryland's bus ride back up Route 29 was far more pleasant than it had been the past two seasons. The Terrapins were now 17–3, 7–1 in the ACC, and looking forward to February.

CHAPTER 8

"I'll Be Ready"

Before the season starts, most of the players in the ACC are familiar with one other. By February and the start of the second half of the double round robin teams play, the players know exactly what to expect from opponents. Nearly every conference game is on television, so players learn one another's on-court tendencies, likes and dislikes, and pet moves.

It's kind of like in the movie *Hoosiers* when the coach played by Gene Hackman tells one of his players to guard an opponent so tight that he will know what flavor gum the guy is chewing. Even when a team isn't playing, its players usually are watching games on television. By this point of the season, even the freshmen have had their games dissected by opponents.

"Watching some teams play, if you see see one guy doing well against another guy, you wonder, 'How did he do that?'" Maryland point guard Steve Blake said. "And seeing teams get more credit than they deserve makes you upset. Throughout the season, you build up a lot of aggression. You want to play well against every team."

As Maryland geared up for the start of the second half of the league schedule, Blake wanted to play especially well. N.C. State was coming to College Park on Sunday, February 3—a game that had been moved up to 4 P.M. so fans could get home in time to watch the Super Bowl.

In the teams' first meeting, Blake and State freshman Julius Hodge had gone after each other throughout. Everyone had heard Hodge talking trash, but few noticed Blake get Hodge in the stomach, sending the ultra-thin freshman to the floor. No way did Blake want to give Hodge, who had been recruited heavily by Maryland, the upper hand in the rematch.

As the teams took the court for the opening tap, Juan Dixon, perhaps the ACC's elder statesman this season, strode past Hodge and told him that his game could stand on its own, that the freshman didn't need to talk to get noticed. "You don't need to do that," Dixon said.

Dixon's words, though, went unheeded, as Hodge continued to yap, and his play, along with Maryland's struggles, helped the Wolfpack take a 57–55 lead midway through the second half.

Quicker than Hodge could get out a few one-liners and tell the Terrapins they weren't so tough, however, Maryland went on another of its trademark runs, scoring sixteen of the next eighteen points. Dixon made a pair of three-pointers and Mouton made two baskets as the Terrapins took control.

While Maryland was nearing its thirteenth consecutive victory at home over the Wolfpack, tensions escalated. Maryland forward Tahj Holden and Hodge exchanged words, and Holden bumped Hodge, prompting State assistant Larry Harris to charge off the bench, only to be held back as diminutive guard Archie Miller grabbed him by his sport jacket.

Official Larry Rose warned Holden and Hodge to knock it off, and soon it was N.C. State coach Herb Sendek erupting. Sendek, one of the most mild-mannered people you will ever meet, thought that center Josh Powell had been fouled on a missed layup, and only a bear hug from Harris restrained Sendek, who was called for his first technical of the season.

And that was just the start of things.

With 45.4 seconds left, N.C. State's Michael Bell made a three-pointer to cut Maryland's lead to 85–73. As the ball went through the basket, Hodge came running down the lane and slammed his right forearm into the back of Blake's head while players gathered underneath the basket for a possible rebound.

Hodge, who later said Blake had started things on the other end of the court, immediately received a technical. Blake, irate, turned and yelled in Hodge's face.

"I was going for a rebound and he elbowed me in the neck," said Hodge, who also accused Blake of landing the undetected cheap shot in the teams' previous meeting. "I retaliated."

Blake denied any wrongdoing.

"The shot went up and I boxed him out," he said. "I guess he thought I boxed him out too hard."

Blake said he was not injured.

"It takes more than that to hurt me," he said, going out of his way to prove his toughness. "He's just a little punk."

Maybe it should not have been a surprise that things boiled over between Blake and Hodge. Both had played on some of the nation's top prep teams and shown off their talents on the national scene before getting to college. Both were intensely competitive. And both did whatever they felt necessary to win the game.

"What makes both guys good is that both have a little bit of chip when they play," Gary Williams said. "They're competitors. After it happens, you can see the personalities and why that can happen."

• • •

Getting through to your ACC basketball coach of choice was nearly impossible on Monday. Concerned after a rash of ugly incidents, the conference had to send a message to its coaches and players. Enough was enough. No more forearms to the back of the head. No more shoves, open- or close-fisted, to the stomach. No more coaches going after players, and no more players acting outlandishly.

Miss Manners could have had a field day with all that had happened in the first five weeks of the ACC season.

Maryland alone was involved in several incidents: Blake and Hodge, Mouton and Wake's Josh Howard, the episode at Virginia. Additionally, there was Krzyzewski's behavior against Georgia Tech. And in Duke's 98–88 victory at Clemson over the weekend, Clemson coach Larry Shyatt had to be held back by his assistant coaches from going after Duke forward Dahntay Jones. After Shyatt had called a timeout, Jones had faced the Clemson bench, posed like a bodybuilder, pointed at the players, and yelled, "You're a bunch of motherfuckers!" according to witnesses.

Nice.

The ACC certainly was not alone in its players' and coaches' misconduct, but it was hardly the way a league that prided itself on its basketball wanted to be perceived.

So on Monday morning, ACC commissioner John Swofford hit the phones. There was a conference call with officials, telling them to call things more closely, particularly player taunting. There was a conference call with the coaches. A letter was sent to school officials.

Shyatt and Virginia assistant coach Walt Fuller were reprimanded. Hodge received a one-game suspension for hitting Blake in the back of the head.

While the ACC sorted through its behavioral issues, Williams had one of his own. He had read Blake's quote calling Hodge "a little punk" and, to say the least, wasn't happy. The last thing he wanted to do was give an opponent any extra motivation. The Terrapins and Wolfpack were done with their regular season series, but they still could meet in the ACC tournament. Before practice, as the players gathered in the team lounge to review the previous day's videotape, Williams delivered a stern lecture.

Coach Gary Williams, here getting his shot off against standout guard Juan Dixon, arrived at the University of Maryland in 1989 and resurrected a troubled program.

The 2001–02 Maryland Terrapins: *(Bottom row, left to right)* Team manager Stephen Wheeler, assistant coach Jimmy Patsos, assistant coach Dave Dickerson, Calvin McCall, Juan Dixon, Lonny Baxter, Byron Mouton, Earl Badu, head coach Gary Williams, assistant coach Matt Kovarik, team manager Nikhil Verma. *(Top row, left to right)* Trainer J. J. Bush, strength-and-conditioning coach Kurtis Shultz, Andre Collins, Mike Grinnon, Ryan Randle, Chris Wilcox, Matt Slaninka,* Tahj Holden, Drew Nicholas, Steve Blake, director of basketball operations Troy Wainwright.

* Slaninka transferred before the season began.

The 2001–02 season was Maryland's last at historic Cole Field House. Over its forty-seven-year history, Cole hosted a number of memorable games—NCAA finals, classic ACC matchups, even legendary high school games. Of all the stars who graced Cole's hardwood, perhaps none produced as many highlights as Len Bias; sadly, Cole was also the site of Bias's memorial service, after the Maryland star died of a cocaine overdose in 1986.

Gary Williams over the years became known for his red-faced tirades and visible tension during games. At crucial points during the championship season, though, Williams suppressed his temper when he knew that an outburst would only deflate his team.

The Terrapins had many opportunities to celebrate in 2001–02, as they compiled a 32–4 record. Here, at the final game at Cole Field House, players Chris Wilcox (#54), Steve Blake, Drew Nicholas, and Lonny Baxter cheer a basket by senior walk-on Earl Badu in the final moments of Maryland's victory over Virginia.

The remarkably athletic Chris Wilcox, above, performed numerous highlight-worthy dunks during the season. The harder you slam it, the more points you get, it seemed Wilcox thought.

Senior Byron Mouton, here slam-dunking against North Carolina, was the team's biggest character, its most outgoing personality. In December, however, Mouton received the tragic news that his brother Kevin had been shot and killed; basketball provided an outlet for him in that difficult time.

The Duke Game
Cole Field House, February 17, 2002

Steve Blake's steal from All-American Jason Williams led to this layup at the end of the first half, which gave the Terrapins a nine-point halftime lead—and the momentum.

Punctuating the victory over the Blue Devils was this long inbounds pass from Chris Wilcox to Juan Dixon, who raced past Duke's Mike Dunleavy for a layup.

Maryland fans mobbed senior center Lonny Baxter after the Terrapins knocked off top-ranked Duke. After several heartbreaking losses to the Blue Devils, Maryland had finally proven that it could beat them—and that it was a legitimate national title contender.

The Maryland team, though laughing and joking just before its opening-round NCAA tournament game against Siena, was undoubtedly serious about its objective: a national championship. The night before the Siena game, Juan Dixon had called a players-only meeting to refocus the Terrapins after their ACC tournament loss to North Carolina State.

In the East Regional final, the Terrapins held off a stiff challenge from UConn. With Maryland trailing with just 3:43 remaining, Dixon nailed this game-tying three-pointer over his defender, Taliek Brown.

In celebration of the Terrapins' second straight trip to the Final Four, the players doused Gary Williams with water. The drenched coach was forced to take off his suit and don backup point guard Andre Collins's warm-ups for the postgame news conference.

Maryland's team had the aura of a rock band on tour, and Juan Dixon was the lead singer, recognized everywhere he went. Fans often waited in hotels, pens in hand, asking for autographs.

In the championship game, matched up against Indiana stopper Dane Fife, Dixon again led—indeed, seemingly willed—the Terrapins to victory. "Your best player, if you are going to win a championship, has to step up and make plays," said Indiana coach Mike Davis. "And he did that."

At last: Juan Dixon and Lonny Baxter, the team leaders, collapse in jubilation after defeating Indiana for Maryland's first national championship.

Dixon, voted the Final Four's most outstanding player, cuts down the net and tosses it to his teammates in celebration.

The pep rally back at Cole Field House was just one of many championship celebrations for the Terrapins, who would be feted in Baltimore, at the Maryland state legislature, at the U.S. Capitol, and ultimately at the White House.

"You've got to watch what you say," Williams said, according to one player who repeated the G-rated version. "It's not right to talk trash to the papers about anybody else."

As Williams spoke, Blake knew the coach's talk was directed his way. "I watch myself," Blake said. "I don't have a problem. I'm not going to lash out in the papers. But if you word something the wrong way, it can be blown up."

• • •

Maryland had the week off, then went to North Carolina and cruised to a 92–77 victory in the Dean Dome. An 85–65 victory over Georgia Tech on February 13 gave the Terrapins seven wins in a row. Dixon had missed all nine of his three-point attempts, but it hardly mattered as Maryland improved to 20–3, 10–1 in the league, with a rematch against Duke looming.

By mid-February, most players are beginning to tire, the result of a long season. Practices seem longer and more tedious; they become drudgery. In Maryland's case, the season had been especially long, starting with the earliest season opener in school history. Yet the Terrapins, now using an eight-man rotation with Ryan Randle joining the seven returning players, seemed fresh as they prepared for the stretch run.

"The good thing about the team was you could practice for an hour and fifteen minutes the day before a game and be very confident that you had done enough things to be ready to play," Gary Williams said. "You might change one or two things because of who we play... but once you went over that in practice, you were done. It didn't take a lot of time to get the game plan in, because it was a veteran team and you knew they would be ready to play."

In previous seasons, the team would spend extra time watching film clips and studying opponents' tendencies. But with such an experienced team, Maryland's players already knew most of the tendencies of their

ACC opponents. And because the Terrapins were playing so well at both ends of the floor and knew what to expect from one another, they had few adjustments to make. Opponents, Williams believed, were the ones who had to adjust to the Terrapins, an unusual thought.

In the days leading up to the Sunday, February 17, game against Duke, however, Maryland decided to make some changes. During practice on Friday, Juan Dixon approached the team's assistant coaches. Dixon was aware that the coaches planned on assigning Byron Mouton to defend Mike Dunleavy and Chris Wilcox to defend Dahntay Jones, just as Maryland had done in the teams' first meeting. Dixon and some teammates, though, had been talking about the matchups and thought that Wilcox, with his size and athleticism, might be better suited to defend the high-scoring Dunleavy. With his height, Wilcox could get a hand in the way of Dunleavy's jump shot while not giving up too much quickness.

Every player has a trademark way to get into a rhythm, and Maryland's players thought Dunleavy's was to make some jump shots, drawing his defender farther away from the basket, and then use his speed to drive to the hole. If Wilcox was on the Duke forward, the players thought, his size might limit Dunleavy's ability to shoot from the outside, since he was accustomed to shooting over shorter defenders.

The assistants told Williams of Dixon's suggestion, and after the coaches conferred, they decided to give it a try. Wilcox would have the challenge of guarding Dunleavy.

Meanwhile, Dixon was trying to make up for his subpar performance at Duke and his oh-fer from long range against Georgia Tech the previous game. Determined to break out of a mini-slump, after relaxing for a few hours after practice he would drive over to Cole and get in some extra shooting, the team managers having left the lights on. Some fans and observers occasionally questioned his shot selection and his dribbling skills, but no one would dare say that Juan Dixon lacked dedication.

"I'll be ready Sunday," Dixon promised. "I missed a lot of open shots [when the teams played in January]. I'm cool."

In addition to his extra shooting, Dixon had been taking one other step to prepare for games. Because defenders had been making a habit of grabbing his shirt to stay close, Dixon began tightly tucking his shirt into his shorts, hoping to make it more noticeable when opponents tried to impede his progress.

While Dixon worried about his ability to make amends for his first performance against Duke, Coach Gary Williams had something much more serious on his mind.

Late Friday night, as Williams relaxed in his Potomac town house, the phone rang. He knew it was one of two things. Either one of the players had gotten in trouble or William Williams, Gary's father, had passed away. William Williams had been in the hospital for about a week, and Gary knew that when an eighty-five-year-old is hospitalized, it often is serious.

When Gary Williams picked up the handset and heard his brother Douglas's voice, he knew what had happened. Instantly, as his brother spoke, Gary began to think about two very different things. On one hand, he reflected on his relationship with his father. In recent years, the two had grown to respect each other, though they never were close. William Williams never could understand his middle son's fascination with sports and never attended games. Gary also thought that if his father had to die, perhaps it had happened in a good way, without his father going through much suffering. "I'm sure he was in better shape than me," Gary said of his father, who had quit smoking after World War II and who in his last years walked several miles daily, ate well, and still was driving. "From that standpoint, his last thirty years were better than most people's last thirty years. He wasn't restricted at any point in his life."

On another level, Gary Williams thought about his team. The Terrapins were about to play one of their biggest games of the season. Sure, they were pretty much guaranteed a spot in the NCAA tournament, but a victory over Duke would prove that Maryland was one of the true contenders for the national title. The team was on a roll and already had dealt with plenty of adversity. Williams quickly decided he would not tell the players until after the game.

"My reaction was pretty typical," he said. "Sometimes you wish you could have been closer or whatever. I didn't cry. If it were more of a shock, I would have. I was sad, because you probably never spent as much time together as you would have liked to. There were times I probably could have seen him more and I didn't. At the same time, I think he knew me better as time went on. He couldn't understand my passion for what I did. To him, I just had a job. It didn't make a difference that it was sports. It was just a job. He never understood the team."

Gary Williams got a paltry three hours of sleep that night as his thoughts vacillated between his father and his team, but he came up with his plan. The funeral was scheduled for Tuesday, meaning that he could run his team through a light practice on Saturday, coach Sunday's game, and then drive to New Jersey on Monday.

When the staff arrived on Saturday morning to get ready for practice, Williams informed them and gave the instructions that his personal loss was not going to affect the team.

• • •

Not in years had a game at Cole Field House been this highly anticipated. Students camped out for days—in the middle of February—then made a mad rush inside the arena to be sure of getting tickets. On the Internet and in classified ads, some folks fortunate enough to have tickets were trying to resell them for more than ten times face value.

On February 17, the old barn was going to have one last hurrah. In the blue corner was number-one Duke, with a record of twenty-three wins—coming mostly by knockout—and just one loss. In the red corner was number-three Maryland, with a record of twenty wins—also mostly by knockout—and only three losses.

Sunday morning started with the standard routine. The players were well rested, having been in their rooms plenty early because of a rare curfew instituted by Williams. Maryland's players did a quick walk-through and then drove over to the Greenbelt Marriott to eat a beefed-up brunch in the hotel's sports bar.

Coach Williams believed in following a set schedule and so did his players. They rarely changed their pregame eating habits and always seemed to play the same jokes on the same people. Blake and Nicholas enjoyed messing with each other, whether it was hiding the other's shoes somewhere in the locker room or, during road trips, hiding the other's room key.

"Whenever you are missing something, you pretty much know who to go to or who to blame," said Calvin McCall, who had the unusual superstition of, after the starting lineups were announced, sticking his chewed spearmint gum on the underside of the chair Williams would sit in during the game.

Virtually every coach in every sport feeds his team the line that no single game is more important than any other game. Williams was no different in the days leading up to the Duke game, insisting that win or lose, life would go on. In this instance, Maryland's players knew that was a bunch of crap. The Terrapins felt the venom their classmates had for Duke. And they knew that the Blue Devils were number one in the country, had handled Maryland one month earlier in Durham, and had delivered the stunning comeback in Cole the previous season.

If there was any question what the atmosphere would be like, it was answered about ninety minutes before tip-off, when Mike Dunleavy Sr., father of the Duke forward, walked down the stairs through the student section to his seats behind the visiting team bench: *"Fuck Dunleavy! Fuck Dunleavy!"* the students chanted.

Maryland's student contingent isn't the friendliest bunch around, a constant thorn in the side of administrators and alumni who would prefer a more respectful crowd. Those folks probably weren't happy with the "Fuck Duke" T-shirts, in at least eight different versions, that were out in force.

"Fuck Dunleavy," though, might have set a new all-time low. The other notable serenade came when the parents of Duke center Carlos Boozer arrived. After the previous season's game at Cole, Renee Boozer, Carlos's mother, had been hit in the head by a thrown water bottle, an incident that focused the spotlight squarely on some fans' poor behavior. Now, as the Boozers walked to their seats, many in the crowd started chanting *"Aquafina,"* the name of the water manufacturer. For Maryland's fans, it was a rare instance in which an attempt at humor won out over vulgarity.

As the stands filled, Maryland's players were joined in their locker room by former standout Steve Francis, now an All-Star with the Houston Rockets. Conveniently, the Rockets were playing at the Washington Wizards the next night, and there was no way the bubbly Francis was going to miss seeing his former school play its hated rival. It was unusual for Williams to bring anyone to address the team before the game. In this instance, though, it seemed only natural for Francis to speak to the players.

And if the Terrapins needed any added incentive, they had it sitting in the corner of the locker room, where two dozen awful-looking black and blue roses sat in a bouquet along with a poem about how Maryland was going to lose. A Duke fan had given the flowers to Maryland trainer J. J. Bush in the parking lot before the game.

For this game, though, the Terrapins were more than ready. Maryland started quickly, with Dixon hitting from the right side, Wilcox making two free throws, and Byron Mouton making a seventeen-footer from the left wing for a 6–0 lead. In the first game, the lead had seesawed back and forth, but it took almost no time to see which team was better on this day. The only official lead change came when Maryland scored the game's first basket.

Dunleavy, guarded by Wilcox, was hot early, scoring ten of Duke's first fourteen points. The problem was, the rest of the Blue Devils might as well have been no-shows. Jason Williams, the splendid point guard, was missing shots and making turnovers. After shooting 62.7 percent from the field in its previous game, a 108–71 victory over N.C. State, Duke couldn't hit much of anything.

Dixon also was struggling, picking up a pair of charges while worrying about whether Dahntay Jones was holding him. Still, Maryland led 25–14 after a tip-in by Mouton, and it was 33–20 after two free throws by Tahj Holden.

Francis, seated near the end of the bench, was ecstatic, waving his arms after some plays, while after others he was crouched over, with both palms on the floor.

A quick 7–0 run got Duke back in the game, but a bank shot from the right wing by Steve Blake pushed Maryland's lead back to 36–29 and gave the Blue Devils a chance to hold for the half's last shot.

End-of-half situations can be worth more than just two or three points. The momentum from a big shot or key miss can change a game in the second half. Maryland's players still remembered the end of the first half earlier in the season at Duke, when Jones threw in a wild shot and the Blue Devils came out firing in the second half.

This day, the final possession of the half would be just as meaningful.

With the clock winding down, Jason Williams stood along the right sideline just across half-court, turning his head and looking back to Duke coach Mike Krzyzewski for instruction.

"Man, he's not even watching me," Blake thought to himself.

Blake had been about fifteen feet away, but he took one or two steps toward Williams, incredulous that Williams would act like no one was guarding him. Then the Duke guard again looked back at Krzyzewski, turning his head so that he no longer could see Blake.

This was too much for Blake. As soon as he saw Williams turn, Blake lurched forward and knocked the ball free toward the Duke basket. The two pushed at each other as Blake got to the loose ball and dribbled ahead. As he jumped for a layup, Blake knew that Williams was going to go for the block, a difficult play but one that the athletic Williams could make. With that in mind, Blake made sure to put extra arc on the ball, lofting it so high that Williams could not reach it.

"I was thinking about a behind-the-back drop pass to Chris," Blake said. "But I thought, 'Oh, man. What if I miss? Everybody is going to be mad.' "

When the ball slipped through the net, Maryland had a 38–29 halftime lead. Byron Mouton, facing the student sections behind the team benches, leaped in the air with both hands raised. Francis, who had moved about three steps onto the court to get a better viewing angle when Blake went the other way, sprinted into the tunnel and made the left turn into the locker room at top speed. It was as though Francis was the one who had made what might be the most memorable shot in years at Cole.

"The situation just set itself up perfectly," Blake said. "It happened so fast. . . . I just took the opportunity and went after it. I just wanted to time it right. I just remember knocking it loose and taking off and going with it."

For Blake, it couldn't have been any sweeter. At home. Against Duke. From Jason Williams, who eventually would be the consensus national player of the year. It was an incredible swing: if Williams had hit a three-pointer, it would have been a four-point game at the half, but instead, because of Blake's play, the margin was nine.

"It would have been great against anybody, but because it was him and Duke, everyone was like, 'Wow, he did it against Jason Williams, the best player in college basketball,'" Blake said. "I guess if you look at it, if it wasn't [against] as well-known a player, everybody would remember that steal against just that guy instead of against Jason Williams."

Of course, a small matter—the second half—remained. And in each of the teams' previous five meetings, the team leading at the half had gone on to lose.

That trend did not hold up. Wilcox started the second half by feeding Baxter for a layup. After Chris Duhon scored for Duke, Blake penetrated and found Baxter for another layup. It was 42–31, and soon Krzyzewski was calling timeout.

Maryland's momentum wasn't broken, though. Williams fed Boozer for a basket and made a jump shot, but Duke couldn't stop Maryland. Wilcox made a put-back and then cut back-door, took a one-handed bounce pass from Blake, and swooped in for a scooping layup. After Williams air-balled a three-pointer from near the top of the key, Dixon made a three-pointer from the right corner, his first three-ball since midway through the second half of the North Carolina game.

It was 49–35 Maryland, and Krzyzewski was quite upset. "You're 23–1, number one in the country, and you're playing like little kids!" he screamed during a television timeout. "You're not fighting for anything."

Indeed, it was stunning. Here was Duke, the team that prided itself on hustle, getting beaten seemingly to every loose ball. And Maryland was on fire. When Wilcox slammed the ball through the basket off a miss by Blake, it was as if he were being careful not to tear down the entire basket. By the time the Terrapins' 20–4 run was over, the lead had ballooned to 64–39 with more than ten minutes left.

At the end of the bench, Francis was more uncomfortable than he had ever been during a game in Cole. He had looked sharp at the start of the game, dressed in a gray suit. As the game wore on and the temperature rose, though, Francis started peeling off layers of clothing. First came the jacket, then the vest. By game's end, he had untucked and unbuttoned his shirt, and he kept saying to anyone who would listen, "I don't remember it being this hot in here when I played."

Of course, when Francis played, he was on the floor in every tight situation and did not have time to think about the temperature. He got to sit on the bench only after the outcome was decided.

In any other game, leading by twenty-five, Maryland would have been in garbage time. Against Duke, however, and with memories of last season's collapse in everybody's mind, there was plenty of tension. Williams knocked down consecutive three-pointers, then made a steal and fed freshman Daniel Ewing for a three-point play to cut the lead to 69–54 with eight minutes left. If the Blue Devils could make up ten points in less than a minute, fifteen points in eight minutes was nothing.

For a change, though, Maryland's lead was safe. Duke got within eleven with two and a half minutes left, but that was as close as it got. Dunleavy fouled out with fifteen points, scoring only five points after his hot start. Williams had made just six of twenty-two shots with six turnovers. "Last month, we tried to take him off the three-point line and it was a little easier for him to penetrate by me," Blake said. "This time, I tried to stay in front of him. What he hurt us with last time was the penetration."

Dixon also had six turnovers, but he made eight of fourteen shots. Blake had made the game-turning steal and basket, and finished with thirteen assists to go with just one turnover. And the hero had been Wilcox, who ably defended Dunleavy and set career highs with twenty-three points and eleven rebounds.

"I think Chris felt by then in his career that there was going to be a mismatch, regardless of who was guarding him," Coach Gary Williams said, sensing that Wilcox had a habit of playing to the level of the competition. "Chris is such a strong inside player. With their starting lineup, Boozer is their only inside player. He was going to score inside. I think he had that confidence by then.

"If you looked at some of the other games, you wouldn't have the same opinion of Wilcox as a player. But he did it at the right time."

Williams remembered back to the improbable comeback at Virginia. It was a picture of Wilcox's steal and thunderous dunk that had made the front page of the *Washington Post* the next morning, a play that was shown over and over on ESPN and the TV news. While Williams wasn't trying to lessen the impact of that play, he pointed out that Wilcox had made only three of ten other shots in that game and had finished with just eight points, playing only twenty minutes because of his ineffectiveness.

"Chris always had that thing, he made the plays not many people could do," Williams said. "It might be one play out of forty plays and the other thirty-nine might not be as good, but he always had a knack for making that big play.

"The thing about Chris that I admire is he probably played best in big games. The Illinois game, he was dominating. The Duke game he was dominating.... A little bit of that is immaturity, where you don't get ready to play every game. You always talk about not judging the competition, but Chris I don't think ever bought into that completely. He knew who we were playing.... He could really focus when he wanted to. That was underrated. He really thought about how he was going to play Dunleavy."

The victory was important for a number of reasons. It gave the Terrapins the outright lead in the ACC standings and a chance to win its first regular season title since 1980. It also put Maryland in position to possibly move up to number one in the polls for the first time in school history. And it proved that Maryland actually was a national contender.

"We knew then that if we could play that way against a team that good, then we could play with anybody," Williams said. "Because they beat us down there, in the second half they beat us good, that was in the back of our minds from that day on. If we got another chance, that would be a measuring stick for us. Once we won, I think we really thought—in a good way—that we were really good. It's one thing to think you're good, but you have to prove you're good. A lot of guys talk, but it doesn't mean anything until you beat somebody that is really good."

The Terrapins had proven it. Now Williams had to attend to his personal business. He had planned to tell the team about his father after the game. The feeling in the locker room, the euphoria that stretched to every corner of the square room, was so great, though, that Williams did not want to bring his players down from their perch. This was a victory the players should savor, Williams thought, and he could continue to deal with things on his own.

"When you coach, you always try to isolate whatever is going on around you and isolate on the game," Williams said. "I've coached long enough and been able to do that. You don't hear a lot of things around you. It's tougher, because it's your father, but you have to do it."

Some players learned about the passing of William Williams in the next day's newspapers. The rest learned when Gary Williams spoke at a team meeting Monday afternoon and informed the players he would not be at practice that day. By then, the players knew their win had not been big enough to leap Kansas in the polls. Maryland was number two, the Jayhawks number one.

• • •

At his father's funeral, Gary Williams saw a lot of relatives and acquaintances he had not seen in quite some time. While he might have wanted to stick around and make up for time missed, Williams knew he had to be back in College Park for practice that afternoon and the plane to Clemson that night.

At this point, when it went on the road, Maryland's team had the aura of a rock band on tour. Juan Dixon, whether he was wearing Maryland gear or not, was the lead singer, recognized everywhere he went. When the team went to eat in hotel meeting rooms, fans often waited outside or by the elevators, pens in hand, asking for autographs.

"What are you going to do?" Williams said. "You don't mind doing it as long as it is for the kids, but when it starts getting sold, that's not the point. The point is if you make a kid happy by signing an autograph, that's great. But not some guy trying to make a hundred dollars over the Internet. But you don't get to pick and choose."

Maryland left Clemson with an 84–68 victory and returned home for Senior Day, a February 24 game against Wake Forest. Typically, schools honor their seniors at the season's final home game, but with Cole Field House closing, it was decided to move the event up and give Dixon, Baxter, Mouton, and Earl Badu their own day.

It was a special day for the tandem of Dixon and Baxter. The two native Marylanders often had been told they would never make it at this level; today, their jerseys would be hung in the rafters, joining a select crowd.

As the jerseys were unrolled, Gary Williams could not watch. Dixon and Baxter were Williams's favorite kind of player, fighting the odds, never giving up, and simply working hard every day. If he could, Williams would keep these two forever.

As number 3 and number 35 were unfurled high above the court, tears began to well in the coach's eyes. Williams was a private person. He accepted that his job made him a public figure, but he tried to keep his personal life separate. Now, surrounded by nearly fifteen thousand people, Williams was about to break down.

If you weren't looking closely, however, you never would have seen it. As soon as the ceremony was over, Williams hightailed it down an aisle and into the locker room. He didn't want anyone to see his emotion.

As for the game, Maryland trailed by as many as twelve points in the second half but rallied. With 1.3 seconds left and the game tied, Wake's Josh Howard called timeout—but the Demon Deacons were out of timeouts. It was a technical foul, and Dixon made one of two free throws. The Terrapins escaped with the win, 90–89.

While the victory might have seemed fortunate, somehow Mouton claimed credit for Howard's error. The two had tangled many times over the past two seasons, and Mouton thought he had been so distracting that he had forced Howard to miss a free throw with ten seconds left and then, after rebounding a miss by Dixon, forget that his team did not have a timeout remaining.

"I was so into that dude's head," Mouton said. "I told him, 'You're going to lose the game for your team.' He missed the free throw and he called timeout. I take some of the credit. I was in that dude's head the whole game."

And so on a day that saw Maryland honor two of its best players for their on-court performances, Mouton said the key ingredient to the team's tenth consecutive win was his ability to play mind games with an opponent.

"I never saw him as a pest or annoying," assistant coach Dave Dickerson said. "I wish that everyone could be like him. I hope my son plays the game as hard and has a love and thirst for the game the way Byron does. Byron did all kinds of things. There are stories. Byron learned the game in the South, playing that street ball. Anything goes. Anything it takes to gain an advantage, an edge, that's what you do. There are all kind of tricks in the game you can do to distract people and Byron knew those things.

"I think every team needs a person that is going to give up some offensive dreams to make the team good in other areas. And that's what Byron did. He gave us that toughness."

• • •

The Terrapins followed the Wake Forest squeaker with a 96–63 pasting of Florida State that was notable only for the nastiness of some students standing courtside behind press row. The Tallahassee–Leon County Civic

Center is a lousy place to play basketball, and with the Seminoles struggling and Coach Steve Robinson about to be fired, the crowd was dreadfully small. That only made the students' profanity-filled taunts seem even louder, and they got the attention of several Maryland players, who nodded in response.

The victory left the Terrapins at 24–3, 14–1 in the ACC, clinching a share of the regular season title and setting up the final game at Cole Field House as a grand celebration.

That celebration actually started about seventy-two hours early, when Virginia upset Duke, 87–84, giving Maryland the regular season title outright. Williams and Dixon, wanting to share the moment with each other, had been on the phone—Dixon in his apartment, Williams in his town house—watching the game together as the Cavaliers rallied to win.

"It's big, especially given the fact Duke had won five straight years," Williams said that night. "You had to believe, you had to have confidence you could do it, and that was tough to do given what they have done."

The Cole finale, a game that already was special for many reasons, would be punctuated by the Terrapins' cutting down the nets.

On March 3, fans started showing up well before tip-off, everyone walking around the narrow concourse to try to recapture fading memories. Lines for game programs stretched halfway around the building. The athletic department had taken several precautions prior to the game, removing all trophies and keepsakes from the trophy cases. To clamp down on counterfeiters, the university had printed the tickets on special, multilayered stock (the middle layer was a different color that showed up only when the ticket was torn); had designed background images on the tickets' back sides that would show up darker in copies and scanned images; and had hand-stamped on the tickets the words "Go Terps" in ink that was visible only under a black light. Doormen were on the lookout for wrenches and other tools fans might try to sneak in to pry loose mementos.

Among those who came back were former Maryland basketball stars Buck Williams, Len Elmore, and Tom McMillen; Boston Celtics coach Jim O'Brien, a former Terrapin assistant; and former Maryland star quarterback Boomer Esiason. Tickets were being scalped for several hundred dollars. No one wanted to miss the show.

The current Terrapins did not disappoint. Trailing 19–14 midway through the first half, Maryland went on another dizzying run, outscoring the Cavaliers 25–5 over the next few minutes. Yet again, Mouton was in the center of controversy, bumping into Virginia's Keith Jenifer (though Mouton later said it was an accident); Jenifer, the same player who had been in the middle of a fracas during the teams' first meeting, retaliated by hitting Mouton in the back of the head and was called for an intentional foul.

"I think he is just trying to start stuff on the low," Jenifer said a few days later. "He gets other players to respond and they're the ones who get in trouble. It works. He got me once."

Said Mouton, "I get a thrill off that, to see guys get mad at the little things. I just do any little thing to get the advantage."

Virginia closed within 43–36 at halftime, but Maryland started the second half with a Blake three-pointer from the top of the key and two free throws by Baxter. Perhaps sensing it was going to be a long night, Virginia coach Pete Gillen sighed to no one in particular, "Way to start the second half."

The Cavaliers never got close. Cole Field House would close just the way it had started, with Maryland beating its neighbor to the south. The final was 112–92. Perhaps the only slipup came when Dixon, not knowing Coach Williams remained, cut the final strand of the net; he quickly retied it when he realized his gaffe.

Maryland had finished the regular season with a twelve-game winning streak and the best record in school history, 25–3 overall, 15–1 in the ACC.

"We're very confident," Blake said. "We have the feeling we can beat anybody at any time. But we know we have to work hard."

Just the way Williams would want it.

CHAPTER 9

The Same Old ACC Tournament

As much as Gary Williams hated the idea, he knew all too well that he and his players would be judged on how they fared in March. He had always felt there was too much emphasis placed on the postseason in measuring a team's success. If Williams had his way, fans, the media, Dick Vitale, and everyone else would judge a team and its coach largely based on its performance during the four-month regular season.

"People seem to think that you're not a good coach unless you reach the Final Four," Williams said. "Well, there are no two better coaches than John Chaney [of Temple] and Gene Keady [of Purdue], and they've never gotten there. Every situation is different, and they've done great jobs in their situations."

In college football, Williams often pointed out each season as the ACC and NCAA tournaments rolled around, some fifty teams play in bowl games, which at many places, including Maryland, is enough to say that a season was worthwhile. Half of those teams win their bowl games, taking home a championship trophy of some sort and ending the season on a positive note.

In college basketball, barring unusual circumstances, only one team wins its final game. Just making it to the NCAA tournament, let alone winning a few rounds, ought to be enough to satisfy the masses, Williams strongly believed.

Of course, the naysayers liked to point out that until the 2000–01 season, Maryland had never done anything truly special in the postseason, so why wouldn't its coach want to put more focus on the regular season? After all, before the 2000–01 season, Maryland was regarded as one of the best programs never to make the Final Four.

When the Terrapins did advance to the Final Four, they made it after one of their shakiest seasons in several years, needing a late-season rally just to earn an NCAA tournament invitation. Nobody really cared, though. The Final Four was the Final Four.

Now the best regular season in Maryland history had to be put aside. Finishing first in the ACC during the regular season for the first time since 1980 was meaningless. It all had to be forgotten. First up was a trip to Charlotte, North Carolina, for the ACC tournament; the NCAA tournament would follow. Four pressure-packed weekends would determine how this Terrapin team would be remembered.

If he was feeling any added stress, though, Juan Dixon did not show it as he greeted a visitor in his off-campus apartment one afternoon before practice.

Aside from Williams, whose paycheck relied on the team's performance, Dixon might have had the most at stake. He was a senior, and in a month or less, his college career would be over. Dixon had been a sensational college player. He could shoot, score, and play defense and was willing to do anything he could to help the team win. He also stayed out of trouble and represented the university well.

The problem was, Dixon knew that many observers thought he was only that: a sensational *college* player. Listed at 6 foot 3, which he might get to on tippy-toes, Dixon lacked the size most NBA scouts want in a shooting guard, and he lacked the ballhandling ability to play point guard in the League. With a strong performance in the postseason, Dixon might persuade some scouts that the intangibles he brought to the table were worth more than a few inches here or there.

He had taped on a wall in his bedroom a two-page printout of one NBA mock draft that had him as a middle second-round pick. To many folks, including Gary Williams, there was not a better collegiate player this season. Some people might argue for Duke's Jason Williams, but who else was there? Surely there couldn't be forty others better than Juan Dixon.

Dixon could not believe that people still doubted him after all he had done at Maryland. What else could he do? On the wall, between the pages, Dixon wrote in capital letters, "MOTIVATION! WORK HARD!" It was more than an issue of—again—proving the doubters wrong; Dixon knew a lot of money hung in the balance. Second-round draft picks are guaranteed nothing and often are cut, forced to the minor leagues or Europe; first-rounders receive guaranteed seven-figure contracts that assure them a place on the roster.

It would have been understandable if Dixon was anxious, knowing what lay ahead. As he prepared for one last postseason run and a chance to improve his own stock, however, he was relaxed as he sat on his neatly made bed and talked. "I've had a good experience," Dixon said. "Me and Drew were just talking about it. This is our year to do it. It doesn't get any better. It's a great opportunity. We've got to take advantage of it.... I just want to enjoy this last month. My college career, everything has happened so fast for me. I barely got a chance to sit back and just think and put everything into perspective. Now it's over already. I can remember the first day I got here."

There wasn't much time to think, though. Practice was in a few minutes, and Dixon had to make the short drive over to Cole as the team prepared for Friday's ACC tournament quarterfinal against either Florida State or Clemson.

• • •

As usual, the ACC tournament was in the Tar Heel State. It always was, or at least it seemed that way to Gary Williams and the rest of Maryland's contingent. Duke, North Carolina, State, and Wake Forest could simply hop on a bus and in two hours or less be at the tournament site. This season, with the tournament in Charlotte instead of its former home in Greensboro, so could Clemson. And perhaps more important, so could the fans of those schools.

The ACC tournament is a wonderful party. It doesn't matter that the teams arrive pretty much knowing whether they are headed for the NCAA tournament and that the ACC tournament, in the grand scheme of things, matters little. The league distributes tickets evenly among the schools, meaning that for Friday's quarterfinal games, no team really has a home-court advantage unless other teams' fans start rooting for the underdog.

By Saturday, though, that changes, as fans of losing teams sell their tickets and head home. Face it, the Florida State and Clemson fans aren't interested in watching Maryland, Duke, and North Carolina. But fans who can drive in for the day and drive home afterward might want those tickets, thereby giving the North Carolina teams an advantage.

"They get the house the way they want it by the time you play on Saturday and Sunday," Williams said. "That tradition, in that state, where the league was founded, is what set it up. And we've always been looked at as the Yankees from the North because we're the northernmost team in the league."

This was the forty-ninth annual ACC tournament; of the forty-three previous ones held in North Carolina, thirty-nine were won by teams from North Carolina. Of course, of the five ACC tournaments not held in North Carolina, the North Carolina teams won three, and Maryland actually had a better winning percentage in tournament games played in North Carolina (.451) than it did in those played in Atlanta, Georgia, and Landover, Maryland (.417). Still, Williams thought it was no accident that Virginia had won the 1976 tournament and Maryland the 1984 tournament, which were held at the old Capital Centre in Landover.

"If you played [the ACC tournament] forty-four of forty-nine times in Baltimore and Ocean City," Williams said, "I think we'd have a little better record.

"Let's face it. The way the conference is set up, there is a reason why no [ACC] team outside of Carolina ever won the national championship in basketball. The league office is from Carolina. There are four teams in there. Now people are starting to realize there are five teams outside the state of North Carolina in the conference."

Indeed, in the summer of 2000, faculty representatives from the nine ACC schools voted to move the league's prized jewel among various sites. Prior commitments had to been fulfilled (Atlanta in 2001, Charlotte in 2002, and Greensboro in 2003 and 2004), but in 2005, the faculty representatives decided, the ACC tournament will be held at Washington's MCI Center, the first time since 1984 it will be staged north of the Virginia–North Carolina state line.

"I always fought for the ACC tournament to be moved around, but the league felt it would hurt the image of the league if it wasn't held in North Carolina," Williams said. "If you play that thing in MCI Center, that's certainly going to be a big three days in 2005. Hopefully, I'm still coaching then."

That might be good for the future—after the 2001 Final Four run, Williams signed a new contract through 2008—but for the present, it was meaningless, as Maryland took its pizza boxes and sodas and headed off to Baltimore-Washington International Airport.

• • •

Having finished first during the regular season, Maryland was the top seed in the tournament and would play in the noon quarterfinal game on Friday, March 8, against the winner of Thursday night's play-in game between Clemson and Florida State. The Terrapins had swept both of those teams during the regular season and didn't really care who won. If Maryland played even average, it figured to have no problem advancing to the semifinals.

"We just want to play well," Williams said Thursday afternoon as the team went through an informal workout at the Charlotte Coliseum. "We've stayed with that all year. If we play well, we're going to be a tough out."

Though no one would dare say it, they had their eyes on a potential meeting in Sunday's championship game with Duke. Maryland was on a roll, having won its past twelve games and played at a high level down the stretch. There was no reason to think the Terrapins and Blue Devils, who clearly were the two best teams in the league, wouldn't get it on a third time this season.

On Friday, Maryland would play Florida State, which had advanced with a 91–84 victory over Clemson on Thursday night.

The Seminoles were the team that nearly wrecked Maryland's season the previous year with the Valentine's Day disaster in Cole Field House. This season, though, they had won only one other game since late January, and, barring a miracle, Coach Steve Robinson almost certainly would be fired.

With fans filing in late, Maryland started slowly against Florida State's 2–3 zone defense. Soon enough, though, the Terrapins went on one of their runs, scoring thirteen consecutive points and taking a 19–7 lead. Byron Mouton was a one-man show. He dunked a fast-break alley-oop pass from Steve Blake, swinging from the rim while pointing back at Blake; he followed misses by Juan Dixon and Blake, and then made a line-drive jumper from the left side.

It was 40–28 at halftime. While the game was not yet a blowout, there was a sense that Maryland could not lose.

That quickly changed after the first few minutes of the second half. Dixon bricked a three-pointer and missed a jumper, Blake committed a turnover, and the Seminoles pulled within eight points, 40–32. Williams, irate that his team had let Florida State back in the game, called a timeout to yell at the players and tried to make a point by throwing his marker.

After the timeout, Dixon made a jumper from the foul line, but Monte Cummings—the Seminoles' twenty-five-year-old army veteran—made two free throws and a layup, and then scored on a drive. It was 42–38, and Williams again signaled for a timeout. This time, the coach was calm, talking to his players and trying to point them in the right direction while replacing Chris Wilcox with Tahj Holden. Naturally, the peaceful approach resulted in a turnover by Blake and a three-point play at the other end for the Seminoles.

Now it was 42–41, and fans from the other schools were pulling for Florida State. As the teams went to their benches for the half's first television timeout, the anticipation was building throughout the arena. Would the number-one seed lose a quarterfinal game for just the third time ever?

Williams could not believe it. Already in the half, he had called two timeouts. He was a ranting madman during the first one and tried the opposite approach during the second. With two more minutes to speak to his players, Williams found another approach: he got up out of the huddle, walked to the end of bench near the baseline, and sat alone, leaning forward with his elbows on his knees.

"He was leaving it up to us to figure out what we needed to do," Blake said. "Sometimes it works. . . . I don't get too surprised with anything he does. It wasn't too shocking to me."

Maybe not, but Williams's theatrics achieved the desired result.

Maryland made seven of its next eight shots. Blake hit a three from the right side to start the run. Mouton followed with two free throws, and Holden was good on a turnaround jumper. Blake swung a pass to Dixon for another three, from the left side, and then Dixon grabbed a rebound, pushed the ball up the court, and found Nicholas for a three-point play.

By the time the stretch was over, the Terrapins had scored twenty-one consecutive points and provided a reminder why they had been so good all season. The final was 85–59.

"We're one of those teams that can make really good spurts really quick," Nicholas said. "Sometimes you don't realize it, because you're in the midst of a game. We don't want to rely on those kind of runs, but that is one of the things that has helped us become the team that we are."

Dixon, Nicholas, and the rest of the team—along with Williams—left the arena to prepare for Saturday's semifinal.

"You can't use that one too often," Williams said of his new timeout approach. "But it worked. I had nothing good to say, so I got out of there. Every once in a while, you have to do something different. We were in a little fog.

"I feel great about this team. It's never going to be smooth. There's some pressure when you're the number-one seed, a lot more pressure than when you're any other seed."

• • •

Saturday's opponent was North Carolina State, which had advanced with a 92–72 quarterfinal victory over Virginia, setting set up another meeting between adversaries Blake and Julius Hodge, who slapped hands with each other as the teams took the court.

While Maryland had spent the past twenty-four hours trying to shake out of the doldrums, against N.C. State the Terrapins resembled the team that had been sleepwalking in the previous day's victory over Florida State. Blake threw a pass between Tahj Holden's hands; Holden was called for an offensive foul; then a Blake pass sailed through Randle's hands. Three possessions, three turnovers. Soon Maryland trailed 24–12.

An 11–0 run got the Terrapins back in the game, and after an 8–0 run that took fifty-five seconds, Maryland had a 31–26 lead and once again seemed in control.

The Terrapins, though, could not keep it up. It was 54–54 with twelve minutes left, but then State went back ahead, an Archie Miller three-pointer making it 60–54. Later, back-to-back three-pointers from the wings by Marcus Melvin and Miller made it 75–64. Wolfpack players were dancing all over the court as Williams called a timeout.

Maryland had been through this before, memories of comebacks against Princeton and Virginia still fresh in everybody's mind. The game could still be won. The Terrapins chipped away at the deficit, getting it to 81–78 on three free throws by Blake with 1:53 left.

Then came the play that sealed the game. After running down the thirty-five-second shot clock, Hodge was caught on the right wing and, with a defender in his face, had to let fly an awkward line drive just before the shot clock hit zero. It was a shot that should have had no chance, but it was right on target; State's lead was now 84–78. Maryland plugged away and had excellent chances to tie, but Nicholas and Dixon missed three-pointers in the closing seconds. The coaches were particularly upset with Nicholas not for his miss but because he had passed up a wide-open look a few passes before taking his shot.

The final was 86–82, Maryland's first loss since January 17 at Duke. The team's winning streak ended one game short of the school record of fourteen.

As Maryland's players headed to their locker room, they passed by the Duke Blue Devils, who were walking to the court to warm up for the second semifinal. The Terrapins had hoped to play Duke in the final and prove once and for all that they were the best team in the ACC, but that wasn't going to happen. While Maryland's players walked with glum looks, a Duke player was overheard to say, "Let's go now," with special emphasis on the last word; some Terrapins grew angry, taking that as somehow rubbing it in that Maryland had lost.

After a loss, the locker room normally is silent, the players wearing gloomy looks that suggest they would strongly prefer not to have to deal with the media's notepads, tape recorders, and video cameras. And this defeat was no exception. There were hushed voices, and almost no one was eating the postgame meal, the six-foot cold-cut subs on a table in the middle of the room.

Typically, Williams would be all over his players, wanting them to feel the pain as much as he did. After losses, while he didn't want the team's confidence to waver, he wanted to build an anger that would last until the players could get to practice the next day and unleash their feelings on the court. On this occasion, though, Williams shared in the belief that if there was ever a good time for a loss, this was it.

Two years ago in Charlotte, playing in Sunday's final for the first time since 1984, the Terrapins had lost to Duke, then watched the selection show in their hotel before flying home. Getting back to campus around eleven on Sunday night, the players and coaches had little time to recharge before departing for Minneapolis on Tuesday afternoon. This year, Maryland could fly back, leisurely watch Sunday's conference championship games, and then get together as a team to learn its destination.

The players had wanted another shot at Duke, but maybe they would be better off saving that intensity for the NCAA tournament.

"We were over it by the time we left the locker room," Williams said. "Really, this might have been my fault coaching. We didn't focus well the whole week. We had made the NCAA tournament and felt we had a good shot at being a number-one seed.

"Normally, you don't want them to forget about [losing]. That's got to eat away at you for a day until you get to practice again. But we had a bigger fish we were looking for."

As in so many other ACC tournaments, the Terrapins were leaving without any hardware. This time, though, it didn't seem like much of a disappointment.

"Lose to N.C. State in North Carolina," Williams said. "Same old crap."

Just in case any folks on the top floor of the Indianapolis Westin were watching, Williams tried to act confident and say that the loss should have no effect on the team's seeding in the NCAA tournament. "Look at what we did for three months," he said. Inside, though, Williams had doubts, wondering if his team had blown its chance for an extremely favorable draw in the one tournament that mattered most.

As it turned out, he needn't have worried. The next night, when the NCAA announced the field for its sixty-five-team tournament, Maryland was named the top-seeded team in the East Region. The Terrapins' first-round opponent would be the winner of the play-in game between Siena and Alcorn State. Better still, Maryland would have to travel just down the road to the MCI Center in Washington.

The loss to N.C. State hadn't hurt a bit. Maryland received its desired seeding and hometown advantage for the first two rounds, and for a change, the Terrapins would not have to leave the Eastern time zone to get where they wanted to go.

The journey was about to begin.

CHAPTER 10

The Journey Begins

The Terrapins were playing just a few miles from campus, but Gary Williams wanted to isolate his players and have them channel all of their energy into basketball. By the time the team set up camp in the downtown Renaissance Hotel, Williams, Juan Dixon, and just about everybody else had handicapped the field and assessed Maryland's chances of winning the NCAA tournament.

The tournament's other number-one seeds were Duke in the South Region, Cincinnati in the West, and Kansas in the Midwest. If everything went according to seeding, the national semifinals would pair Maryland and Kansas, Duke and Cincinnati.

The Terrapins of course were familiar with Duke, and most of the players had watched Kansas on television several times during the season, knowing that the Jayhawks were considered one of the nation's elite teams. Maryland also knew plenty about Oklahoma—a number-two seed that generally was regarded as among the strongest national title contenders—having lost to the Sooners back in December.

"Honestly, I thought we were as good as anybody," Williams said. "I always think there are maybe twelve or fifteen teams every year, given the fact that they get better during the season, that could win it. There were periods this year where I thought Cincinnati was the best team. I thought when Duke was making their threes, they're very good. Watching a team on TV is a little scary sometimes—I always think teams look better on TV. Kansas looked great. Oklahoma kicked our butt. They had the best athletic ability of any team we played."

For now, though, there was no time to focus on those teams. Maryland's opening game would be Friday, March 15, against Siena. The Saints had been 12–18 during the regular season, but they won four games in four days to win the Metro Atlantic Athletic Conference tournament and then beat Alcorn State, 81–77, in the NCAA tournament play-in game. The five-game winning streak was Siena's longest of the season, and Williams was concerned that the Saints might be the team with momentum, especially when he considered that Maryland was coming off a loss.

Dixon, too, had concerns. After the loss to North Carolina State, he had hinted that not everyone was on the same page. "Maybe guys will commit a little more to the team the next couple of weeks," he said.

On Thursday night, the Terrapins went about business as usual. There was a team dinner in a hotel meeting room, then a nighttime meeting in Coach Williams's room.

When the players returned to their rooms, though, Dixon phoned his teammates and ordered them to come to the room he shared with Drew Nicholas.

The past week had been as tumultuous a time as the Terrapins had experienced all season. Until the loss to N.C. State, Maryland had not felt defeat since mid-January. Confidence might have been at an all-time high, perhaps too high. Some players were putting themselves first and the team second, worrying about who was getting shots and playing time and who wasn't, one player said.

Dixon knew it and he wanted to put an end to it before anything costly happened. He did not want to look back and think about what might have been.

"The NCAA tournament is like the NFL—it's one and done," Williams said. "Play a bad game and you go home in the playoffs. And just to make the playoffs is not enough. What you have to do now is win. In football, if you make a bowl game, that usually is good enough. Where we are in basketball now, in the ACC, if you make the NCAA tournament—which has gotten harder to do—that's not good enough. And sometimes with expectations, if you get to the Sweet Sixteen, that's not good enough either."

With his teammates sitting on the beds, on chairs, and on the floor, Dixon assumed the role of captain. He stood in the middle of Room 556 and conducted a twenty-minute team meeting during which no one else spoke. Dixon went through every player on the team and that player's role for the next three weeks. They were going to straighten things out.

"This is my last time through it," Dixon later explained. "If I have to step up sometime and be more vocal and say things guys might not like, I'm going to say what I have to, because I know what it takes to get back there. Stay positive, that's our main goal, and just believe in each other."

Williams, back in his room with the coaches, eventually learned of the players-only meeting, but didn't think much of it.

"I just heard that they had one," Williams said. "I'm not usually big on team meetings. With somebody like Juan or Lonny, your seniors, by that time there is a tremendous amount of trust both ways. I wouldn't mind Juan Dixon calling a team meeting."

Williams was uninterested in a lot of things teams try to do to motivate themselves. True, the previous year, he had written "MINNEAPOLIS" on a piece of paper and tacked it onto the bulletin board in the corner of the team's locker room to remind the players of that season's Final Four site. But that was the exception; normally, he preferred to avoid such motivational tactics, including putting signs in the locker room or forcing players to fake enthusiasm.

"To me, that's always false," Williams said. "It's like when a coach blows his whistle and ends practice. If a guy wants to clap coming into the huddle, that's fine. But I don't want guys to feel like the coach is watching to see who claps. If you have to do that, what's the purpose? I'd rather have guys who do it on the court. That's leadership, when you put it out there every day. That's what I liked about [quarterback] Shaun Hill on the football team. He did it every day, whatever it was, he did it."

In addition to taking charge off the court, Dixon felt a need to set an example on the court—just as he had during the critical juncture of the previous season, when he put the onus on himself after the loss to Florida State. "I need to be more of a leader," he said.

Some might have wondered just what else Dixon planned to do. He scored, played defense, hustled, and encouraged his teammates.

As the team prepared for its opening game, though, Dixon became more serious. Teammates noticed him limiting his joking around in the locker room and keeping more to himself. The two hours in the locker room before a game can be a long time to kill, but Dixon felt he needed all the time he could get.

"The funny thing was that it started to rub off on everybody," senior Earl Badu said. "Everybody started to get a lot more focused earlier before the game. That's a reflection of a leader. Guys definitely fed off of Juan. I definitely saw guys looking to Juan for leadership. Everybody is different in the way they look to him. If you're an observer, you observe, and definitely on occasion, you could catch guys staring at Juan."

On the court, Dixon was more assertive than he had been all season. He started the Siena game with two free throws, then made a steal and went coast-to-coast for a bank shot, and curled in the lane, took a pass from Blake, and made a jumper. Two three-pointers from the left corner soon followed, and in just over four minutes, Dixon had scored twelve points and Maryland led 18–10.

"I've seen a lot of guys go through the program who didn't finish up strong. I want to know I finished up being aggressive," Dixon said. "Like Laron Profit and Terrell Stokes, how did they finish? Losing to a St. John's team we certainly were more talented than. . . . I wish they could have gone out differently. I just try to learn from those guys.

"I remember what it was like and I don't want to experience that. I think we have a great opportunity to do some great things. I just want to provide leadership and lead by example. If I'm aggressive, I think the team feeds off my energy, feeds off the plays I make on the court, and we play better."

Still, while their star was on top of his game, the Terrapins could not put away the Saints. The lead was only 21–19 before an 11–2 run that helped Maryland take a 52–38 halftime lead. And when Siena scored the first four points of the second half, Williams was irate and called timeout.

Dixon responded, making a sixteen-foot pull-up jumper. Then Blake hit from the foul line in transition and fed Dixon for a long two-pointer. Another Blake-to-Dixon basket made it 60–42, and the Terrapins were on their way. Siena made one brief run, getting it to 79–65 with a minute and a half left, prompting Williams to tell Dixon to take off his warm-up shirt and reenter the game. It was a symbolic move—there was no real threat to Maryland's lead—and the message was clear to the rest of the team: no one was to take it easy.

Though he didn't say it, Williams might have been particularly upset with Chris Wilcox, who played twenty-five minutes and finished with just seven points and four rebounds; at one point in the second half, he attempted the first three-point field goal of his career. It was a near repeat of a game late in the regular season, when Wilcox had only eight points and one rebound in nineteen minutes of an easy victory at Florida State.

"Guys are playing hard when they want to play hard," Dixon said. "But you can't be like that. Guys have got to play forty minutes. We've got to be consistent."

Dixon finished with twenty-nine points, matching his season high, and the Terrapins advanced to the second round with an 85–70 victory. The pressure of becoming the victim of the greatest upset in NCAA tournament history was off: with Maryland's victory, top seeds were now 68–0 in first-round games since the tournament expanded to a sixty-four- or sixty-five-team field in 1985.

"A number-one seed has never lost in a thousand games," Williams said. "We're the last number-one seed to play and we hear all that crap.

"How do you explain it if you lose this one? That's the situation you're facing. Nobody has ever lost this game. So what are you going to say? Do you say, 'I'm going to Mexico,' to get out of here? You don't say you're going to Disneyland. I know that."

• • •

Next in Maryland's path was eighth-seeded Wisconsin, which had advanced with an 80–70 victory over ninth-seeded St. John's.

The Terrapins were familiar with the Badgers from the previous season, when the teams played in Milwaukee in the ACC/Big Ten Challenge. Wisconsin had won in overtime, 78–75, in its final game under Coach Dick Bennett, who resigned after the game, saying his heart just wasn't in it anymore.

Wisconsin had many of the same players, including standout guard Kirk Penney, but the Badgers' style had changed somewhat. And scouting the Badgers was challenging, because they had played just three games in nearly a month: a February 27 victory over Michigan, a first-round loss to Iowa in the Big Ten tournament on March 8, and the victory over St. John's. It was no longer the regular season, when the coaches and players knew pretty much everything about every opponent before even watching film. Now the assistant coaches had some serious studying to do. They would be up until 3:30 each night trying to put together a game plan.

"The biggest thing is trying to get their tendencies," assistant coach Dave Dickerson said. "You can't know everything they do, but you can know their tendencies and their individual tendencies."

With only one day between games, Williams's biggest order was for the players to get rest, since he anticipated a physical game against a talented opponent. He didn't want to work them so hard in practice that they wouldn't have enough left in the tank for a close game. "You just hope somewhere along the line, things sink in," Williams said.

For nearly a half, Wisconsin proved a formidable opponent. Maryland's lead at intermission was 38–30, the biggest news of the night coming when Dixon made a three-pointer from the left wing to break Len Bias's all-time school scoring record. It was a feat that set off rousing applause from the partisan MCI Center crowd, but it was only a hint of what was to come after halftime.

Wilcox started the half with a tip-in, and then Lonny Baxter found Dixon open for a three-pointer from the right wing. Blake found Dixon in transition for a bank shot, and it was 45–30. Then Baxter blocked consecutive shots and Blake made a long pass to Wilcox for a reverse layup. The rout was on.

After Charlie Wills finally got Wisconsin on the board in the second half with a three-pointer, Dixon went on a personal 8–0 run. He made a runner while being fouled, then stole a cross-court pass and made a layup, and finished things off with a pull-up three-pointer from the top of the key—while being fouled. It was 55–33.

"When we play like that, we don't think a lot of teams can play with us," Nicholas said. "And the few that can have a hard time withstanding our punch. We're not trying to be cocky, but that's the way we feel."

Dixon again finished with twenty-nine points, and the Terrapins moved on with an 87–57 victory, their most lopsided ever in NCAA tournament play. He now had 2,172 points in his career, moving past Bias's mark of 2,149.

"It's a great accomplishment, especially in my situation," Dixon said. "Coming to Maryland, a lot of people knocked Gary Williams for recruiting me. I wanted to go out there and prove a lot of those critics wrong. I just went out there and worked hard. I didn't get a chance to watch Len Bias much, but I know he was a great player."

Another Terrapin with a chance to become a great player was Wilcox; few his size rivaled him in terms of athletic ability. Having been challenged by just about everyone in the locker room after his lackadaisical effort against Siena, Wilcox responded with eighteen points and seven rebounds against Wisconsin.

"If I come ready to play, we're a hard team to stop," Wilcox said, leading some to wonder why he didn't come ready to play all the time.

"It's keyed by his rebounding," Tahj Holden said. "If he's above the rim, he's in the game. But sometimes he doesn't jump or get up."

While no one was certain what to expect from Wilcox, Dixon had delivered as he said he would. In two tournament games, he had been nothing short of sensational, doing everything he said he would to lead his team to victory. Dixon was vocal in the locker room and led by example on the court, quietly becoming the most aggressive player in the tournament. He was approaching each game as if it were his last—which, indeed, it could have been, at least in college—from the way he was during warm-ups to the way he conducted himself on the court.

"I wish I could have been doing this the whole year—I probably could have had a better year," said Dixon, who earlier in the week had been named the ACC player of the year, besting Duke's Jason Williams for the award. "It's cool, though. I'm pleased with my year.

"I'm going to do whatever it takes to win. It's the same Juan Dixon, I'm just taking a different approach. I'm trying to start off the game aggressively."

With Dixon steering the turtle machine, Maryland had advanced to the tournament's second weekend and would travel to Syracuse for a Round of Sixteen game against fourth-seeded Kentucky, another team the Terrapins were quite familiar with, because they had played the Wildcats three times in the previous three seasons. The winner would face the Connecticut–Southern Illinois winner for the right to go to Atlanta and the Final Four.

Kentucky was a traditional power playing its best basketball of the season, and UConn also was on the rise. The Terrapins, though, seemed to have regained the swagger and confidence that they lost after the N.C. State defeat.

"I thought we earned the right to be confident. That's why I said what I said at Midnight Madness," Williams remarked, referring to his bold proclamation back in October that the team's goal was the national championship. "I was kind of messing around a little bit, but at the same time I wanted the players to know I thought we could do that. I wanted to make sure they had no other goals than winning the NCAA tournament."

CHAPTER 11

Moving On

By the time the bus had made the short trip from the MCI Center back to College Park, Maryland's coaching staff was ready to start breaking down the team's next opponent, the Kentucky Wildcats.

The team's video staff had acquired videotapes of about ten Kentucky games, including the Wildcats' tournament victories over Valparaiso (83–68) and Tulsa (87–82). In previous years, Maryland's coaches could have scouted those games in person, but the NCAA's new "pod" system—designed to keep more teams closer to home—had Kentucky playing its opening weekend in St. Louis.

Although Kentucky was the East Region's fourth seed, Gary Williams and his staff were particularly concerned. The Wildcats had been through their most difficult season in more than a decade, with players involved in so many incidents that it was tough to keep track.

Players had been caught with fake IDs and had cut classes, skipped practices, and missed curfews. Teammates had fought on a charter plane that had stopped to refuel. One player had protested a lack of playing time by staging a nonshooting protest, which seemed simply laughable.

Another had transferred to a hated rival. To top it all off, an opposing coach had called Kentucky coach Tubby Smith a snitch for pointing out an infraction to the Southeastern Conference office, getting the offender suspended.

That wasn't all.

Center Jason Parker had torn knee ligaments while horsing around in the locker room before Midnight Madness and missed the season. Guard J. P. Blevins had sprained his ankle and broken his wrist, missing chunks of playing time. Swingman Keith Bogans, the former DeMatha High standout who had led the team in scoring in 2000–01 and had considered entering the NBA draft, had been benched twice and been mired in an awful slump.

Yet for everything that had gone wrong, Kentucky had put things together at just the right time. The Wildcats had a star in 6-foot-9-inch forward Tayshaun Prince, a silky-smooth player who could shoot from the outside or take it to the hole; he had scored forty-one points in the victory over Tulsa. Bogans was bouncing back. And Kentucky had a host of big players to bang inside with Maryland's foursome. The Wildcats also had tradition, having won seven national championships, and seemed to have plenty of momentum.

To Maryland, Kentucky was 2–0.

"They were good," Maryland assistant coach Dave Dickerson said. "They could beat us. They had Tayshaun Prince, who was probably playing as well as anyone in the country. And they had Tubby Smith, probably one of the best coaches in college basketball. They were a scary team to play against.

"We had to outexecute them. Even though they were a big team, we had to get the ball inside to open up the outside. The good thing about this year was we didn't have to change anything for anyone. We just had to play our game. It was, 'Hey, let's put our system out there and we have a chance to win the game.'"

As the team headed to Syracuse, New York—with extra hats, gloves, and scarves in tow for the cold weather—interest in Dickerson was heating up. Like most assistants, Dickerson yearned for the chance to run his own program. Nearing the end of his twelfth season as an assistant, he might finally get a chance, it seemed.

For the past month, Dickerson had been hearing from contacts at Radford University, who had been trying to gauge his interest in their head coaching position should it become available—which happened when Radford's coach, one-time Lefty Driesell assistant Ron Bradley, resigned on March 21.

Dickerson was not overly interested in that job, but he was curious about the vacancy at the College of Charleston, where longtime coach John Kresse had resigned on March 12. Going to Charleston would allow Dickerson to move closer to his hometown of Olar, South Carolina, and it was considered a pretty good job for the midmajor level. Kresse had won 560 games in twenty-three seasons, guiding the team to Division I status, making the NCAA tournament four times, and beating Maryland in the 1997 first round.

It was worth learning more, Dickerson decided, though he quickly stipulated that any formal interviews or fact finding would have to wait until after Maryland's season was completed. Like Williams, Dickerson did not want anything to interrupt the team's roll and jeopardize its chance of making it to Atlanta.

That Thursday night, after the Terrapins went through one final practice, the players settled into their rooms in the Embassy Suites. Around a quarter to ten, a large cheer erupted seemingly from every part of the hotel. Duke, the team Maryland still considered its chief opposition in its pursuit of the national title, had been stunned by Indiana, 74–73.

And with that, the team to beat became Maryland.

• • •

On Friday morning, the snow, blowing through the wind in sheets, finally stopped after depositing several inches in upstate New York. But the break in precipitation and the occasional sunshine did not affect Gary Williams, who was seething as he went through his final preparations for that night's game.

That morning's *Washington Post* had had a front-page story about the Maryland basketball team's low graduation rates, reporting that only one of four Maryland players recruited out of high school earned their degrees. According to the NCAA's latest published statistics, for the four-year period from 1991–92 through 1994–95, Maryland players graduated at a rate of 19 percent, worst among ACC teams and well below the national average of 35 percent, the *Post* reported.

To Williams, it was incomprehensible that on the day of one of Maryland's biggest games, a hometown paper had written a story so critical of his team. "Yellow journalism," he angrily labeled it a few days later.

Williams also didn't like the way the NCAA calculated its graduation rates, because players who were in good academic standing but left school early for the NBA counted against the school, as did players who transferred. Players who transferred into a school, walk-ons, and midyear enrollees did not count in the NCAA's calculations. Maryland's most recent and current players were graduating at a higher rate, Williams argued. That information also was in the *Post*'s story.

Williams, though, would have to put aside his displeasure for at least a little while.

For now, Kentucky was top priority. As had been the case the previous week, the Terrapins were the second game of the doubleheader and would not tip off until 10 P.M. Second-seeded Connecticut held off pesky eleventh-seeded Southern Illinois, 71–59, in the night's first game, setting up a rematch if Maryland could advance.

Although the Wildcats were hot and had talented players, the Terrapins' game plan strayed little from its normal course. As always, the key item was getting the ball inside to Lonny Baxter and Chris Wilcox, hoping that would create some open space on the perimeter for Juan Dixon. Dixon would be matched up against Keith Bogans, while Byron Mouton had the assignment of slowing down Tayshaun Prince.

When Maryland started slowly, things did not look good, especially after the streaky Bogans canned a pair of three-pointers in the game's opening minutes and soon converted a fast-break three-point play.

Just as Maryland had feared, Bogans came out on top of his game, while Prince continued his prolific ways. After a three-pointer from the right side by Prince, Kentucky led 19–14 and the nearly fifty thousand people crammed into the Carrier Dome could sense a long night for the top seed.

Dixon and Drew Nicholas soon made three-pointers to put Maryland back in front, but Kentucky would not go away, helped by an uncharacteristically poor night by Blake. Seven minutes into the second half, Marquis Estill dunked and Prince made a jumper from along the right baseline. It was 51–51.

It was an offensive nightmare for the Terrapins, who had been held under eighty-two points just once since New Year's Day. A few minutes later, Mouton jacked up a terrible shot on the fast break, Dixon air-balled a three-point try, and Ryan Randle had his layup attempt blocked.

The pressure was mounting.

"There were a lot of tense moments where every play we had, it felt like the most important part of the game," Tahj Holden said. "It was that kind of game."

It was then, though, that Nicholas delivered the night's biggest shot. Nicholas had come through in other clutch situations, so it did not seem out of the ordinary when, midway through the second half, he came around a pick, took a pass from Blake near the top of the key, and lofted a three-pointer over Prince's outstretched hand. When the ball went through the basket, Maryland had a 56–53 lead.

"I had the open shot," Nicholas said. "I hit it."

In addition to putting the Terrapins back in front, Nicholas's shot gave the offense a brief jump start. Wilcox made a jumper in the lane, fed Baxter for a bank shot, and then made a turnaround jumper from the left baseline. Mouton made a put-back, and Baxter was credited with a basket on a goaltending call. Just like that, Maryland had scored on five consecutive possessions, and it was 64–57.

The Terrapins could not put the game away, but Kentucky never rallied, twice missing the front end of one-and-ones. Maryland held on for its sixteenth victory in seventeen games, 78–68.

"We struggled on offense a little bit, I have no problem saying that," Nicholas said. "When it gets down to this point of the season, you do anything you can do to win—scratch, claw, bite. . . . We won and we advanced."

Standing inside the spacious football locker room after the game, Steve Blake patiently answered every question, though they all seemed similar. *What happened? How could you play like that? Why were you off?*

In thirty-one minutes, Blake had made only two of nine shots, missing all three of his three-point attempts, with just five assists to four turnovers.

"You saw the way I played—I played like crap," Blake blurted out in his typical straightforward manner. "Other guys stepped up. That made the difference. I just couldn't get going. I was short on passes, missed easy shots. It just wasn't clicking tonight.

"I didn't play well at all. I'm upset with myself. But I'm happy we won the game. I'm not going to play this bad again."

While the questions persisted for Blake, he actually had gotten off rather easily. The game ended past midnight, and most of the newspaper reporters writing about the game were up against deadline, with enough time to get just one or two quotes and jam them in their story for the following day's papers. Few of the TV folks needed anything; the local news broadcasts, with the exception of CBS affiliates, were long completed, and the TV crews could get their sound bites the following day, when all attention would be on Connecticut.

Williams, though, was annoyed that the NCAA still wanted to conduct its regular postgame drug testing. After all, with less than forty-eight hours to prepare for the game that would determine how Maryland's season would be judged, why wait until 12:30 in the morning to get a few players to pee in a cup?

• • •

Unlike the previous weekend, when a near all-nighter was necessary for the coaches to prepare for Wisconsin, preparation for UConn was fairly routine. Since the teams had played in the BB&T Classic final on December 3, a 77–65 Maryland victory, the Terrapins already had a game plan for the Huskies.

But while UConn's personnel was the same, the Huskies were a much different team from the one that went to the MCI Center in December. UConn was riding a twelve-game winning streak into its rematch with the Terrapins. Center Emeka Okafor had matured into even more of a presence inside, and fellow freshman Ben Gordon was becoming a big-time shooter.

The biggest change for the Huskies, though, was the dominance of Caron Butler. The small forward might have been the best player in the NCAA tournament, scoring in any manner possible and taking over games. Maryland's game plan was to put Mouton on Butler straight up.

"I felt if I contained him, we were going to blow them out," Mouton said. "I didn't think anybody else on that team was capable of stepping up and putting up big numbers."

For one half, Mouton did a good job, holding Butler to six points. When Tahj Holden made a three-pointer to close the half—just as he had the previous year in the regional final against Stanford—the Terrapins led 44–37.

In UConn's locker room, Coach Jim Calhoun was all over his players, especially Butler, who had been in foul trouble.

"It's your ball club and you can't let them down!" Calhoun yelled, according to Butler; recalling the event, the sophomore held his open palm about two inches in front of his nose to show just how in-your-face Calhoun had gotten.

As the Huskies went back out for the second half, Calhoun pulled Butler aside for one last motivational screamathon. "I was one of the last ones out of the locker room," Butler later noted, remembering that he had gotten to the court so late that he hadn't had time to take any warm-up shots.

Wilcox started the second half by missing a jump hook, while at the other end Butler made a three-pointer from the right wing. Tony Robertson made a layup, and then Butler made another three-pointer, this one from the left side. Maryland's 3–2 zone defense, so effective at the end of the first half, was not working at all.

"We came out zone and he came out with a vengeance," Mouton said. "Oh my God."

In truth, it probably made no difference what defense Maryland was playing. Great players do their best work in critical situations. Having just been challenged by Calhoun, Butler was responding with a big "*Take that!*"

Indeed, even after the Terrapins came out of their zone and went back to man-to-man, Butler stayed hot. He made a fifteen-footer from along the right baseline, then a three-pointer from the left wing as Mouton desperately tried to get in the way. After trailing by seven at halftime, the Huskies had a 54–53 lead with thirteen minutes left.

"He was already a great player, but we just boosted his confidence five or ten notches higher," Mouton said. "He was unstoppable. We couldn't do anything with him. He was getting offensive rebounds, hitting threes, slashing to the goal. He was doing everything."

And Butler, Mouton said, was letting everybody know about it.

"He would talk to the crowd: 'Yeah, bring it!'" Mouton said. "He was already pissed off."

Baxter answered with some free throws, and then Nicholas—in the game for Blake, who again was struggling—pushed the ball up the court and fed Wilcox for a dunk; it was 58–56, Maryland. The lead swayed back and forth until Butler and Taliek Brown made layups to put UConn ahead 75–72 with 4:52 left, causing Williams to call a timeout and put his team back in the zone defense. The man-to-man obviously wasn't working, so why not?

Baxter was fouled and made two free throws, but at the other end Gordon penetrated and found Butler, who was fouled and made two free throws. Maryland was down 77–74 with four minutes left.

Williams was beside himself, yelling at his players and, going back to an old trick, at the alternate official seated at the scorer's table. The Terrapins were so close to making it back to the Final Four, but there was a growing feeling that the Huskies weren't going to let it happen.

In a matter of seconds, though, that changed. Dixon—who was so fired up that earlier he had given a rare show of emotion, clenching his fists after making a shot—pretended he was not going to shoot to get his defender, Brown, to relax. As soon as Brown lay back, Dixon let fly a three-pointer from the top of the key, tying it at 77–77. Then Dixon made two free throws and Baxter posted up for yet another right-side, right-handed bank shot, and Maryland led 81–79.

UConn called timeout, but with the shot clock running down, Brown missed a tough jumper from the left corner of the lane with ninety seconds left. It would prove to be a critical miss.

With everyone in the upper deck standing in anticipation, Dixon drove and fed Baxter, who was fouled and swished both free throws. After Okafor was fouled and made one of two free throws, Maryland had the ball and an 83–80 lead with 56.4 seconds left. The Terrapins ran some time off the clock, then called timeout to set up a play.

"We were going to run a screen-and-roll, with Juan coming off the screen," Blake said.

Although the play was designed for Dixon, Blake—who had missed his only two shots of the game, one of which Okafor had swatted back to half-court—told his teammates that he was going to look to shoot.

It seemed ludicrous. Here he was, playing perhaps the worst weekend of his career, and Steve Blake wanted to take the shot?

"I felt as though I was getting open," Blake said, "and I could get a shot. . . . I didn't even think about it, why I said it. I just naturally said it. I guess it does take a lot of nerve to say something like that. I didn't even think about it. It just came out."

Surprisingly, no one said anything to deter Blake. Blake had not been playing well, but he still had the trust of everyone on the bench.

"Having the ball in Juan Dixon's hands is not a bad thing," Dave Dickerson said. "But Steve Blake is as tough mentally as any player I've ever coached. He's had some bad games at Maryland, but he's always bounced back. He's never let us down. You've got to respect that about him."

Blake would not let anyone down this time, either. He took the inbounds pass out high, and as he dribbled to his right, the play broke down. He gave a shot fake that sent Robertson flying past, then rose and shot a three-pointer that went through the basket with 25.4 seconds left. It was 86–80, and finally Maryland had shaken UConn.

"Everything happened within a few seconds," Blake said. "I'm not thinking, 'Oh my God, if I miss I'm going to be in trouble.' I'm taking the shot because I know I can make it."

When the final seconds ticked off, Maryland had a 90–82 victory and a return ticket to the Final Four. The celebration was not nearly as crazy as it had been the previous year, when the Terrapins secured their first-ever berth in the national semifinals, but it was pretty raucous. Dixon hugged university president C. D. "Dan" Mote, then climbed on Tahj Holden for a piggyback ride. "You've gotta believe, fellas!" Dixon shouted.

As the ladders were assembled to cut down the nets and his teammates were cavorting all over the court, Dixon sat alone on top of the scorer's table. For the past two weeks, he had set his mind on getting the team back to the Final Four. Now he had done it and wanted to soak everything in. A few tears formed in his eyes and slid down his face.

"I probably have never experienced a game like this before," Dixon said. "I've played in a lot of great games, but not with this much on the line."

When it came his turn to snip a piece of the net, Dixon slowly walked to the ladder and—having learned from the final game at Cole—left one piece for Williams. The coach went next, cutting the final strand, then handing the net to Dixon, who insisted on having Williams wear it like a lei.

Maryland was going back to the Final Four, eager to take care of some unfinished business.

CHAPTER 12

At Last

Caught in the middle of a city swarming with basketball fanatics, Gary Williams found refuge in the back of a coffee shop.

Thursday night was the last chance coaches and players had to relax before the big event. Friday would be the final day for practice and interviews. Then, on Saturday, Williams and the players would spend much of the afternoon trying to ease the nervous anticipation that naturally would come before one of the most important basketball games of their lives.

On this night, though, Williams had had time to stop in at ESPN's college basketball awards show at Georgia Tech, where Juan Dixon was named the shooting guard of the year. Williams also was going to attend the NCAA's Final Four Salute, the official kickoff for the weekend hosted by CBS's Jim Nantz and featuring the head coaches of the four teams remaining in the tournament.

Team publicist Kevin Messenger had Williams's itinerary carefully mapped out, making sure the coach would be in the right place by the right time. The last thing Messenger wanted was to screw up the schedule, so earlier he had scouted the fastest route from Georgia Tech, in midtown Atlanta, to the Fox Theatre, just a few miles away, downtown.

In fact, Messenger had done such a good job planning that he and Williams were left with an hour to kill before the Salute started. The downtown area was teeming with fans, media, administrators, and fellow coaches; the Fox Theatre was walking distance from the Hyatt, the Marriott, and the Hilton—the headquarters for, respectively, the NCAA, the media, and the National Association of Basketball Coaches, which holds its annual convention in conjunction with the Final Four. Everywhere you walked, there were reminders of the games—people asking for autographs and scalpers selling tickets.

With nowhere to go and nothing to do, Messenger and Williams got some coffee and pored over the *Atlanta Journal-Constitution.*

"I checked before we went in there and there weren't many people. I thought we had a chance" to go unnoticed, said Williams, who was used to scouting opponents, not coffee shops. "Sometimes you get a lot of artsy people in Starbucks, too. I don't think they really care about the Final Four. Nobody said anything [to us]. That was good, because it's hectic at the Final Four."

In the middle of Atlanta, on the main drag of Peachtree Street, surrounded by people who were there to see the games, Williams could enjoy a few moments of peace before the storm restarted.

"I'm one of the few that go into Starbucks and get coffee," he said. "Get my black coffee and that's it. None of those eight-name drinks."

Gary Williams might be making seven figures, but he was still the rugged Jersey guy who liked his coffee plain and strong.

• • •

That Maryland was joined in Atlanta by the Kansas Jayhawks and Oklahoma Sooners was not surprising. The presence of the Indiana Hoosiers, though, was astounding.

Seeded fifth in the South Region, Indiana had been a popular pick in many office pools to be upset in the first round by Utah. But the Hoosiers, now led by Coach Mike Davis, knocked off the Utes, then handled North Carolina–Wilmington and stunned Duke, 74–73, in the Round of Sixteen. Indiana then beat Kent State, 81–69, in the regional final.

Although the Hoosiers had shocked Duke, they were considered the least likely team to take home the championship trophy on Monday night. Indiana's three other tournament victories had come against double-digit seeds. It was generally thought that Oklahoma would trample Indiana in Saturday night's first semifinal, and then Maryland and Kansas would duke it out for the right to play in the championship game.

The Terrapins and Jayhawks were regarded as two of the nation's top three teams throughout the regular season. When Dixon and Earl Badu watched games in their apartment during the season, they took notice of Kansas, one of the handful of teams Maryland's players and coaches thought had a legitimate chance to win the national championship. The Jayhawks had a star in forward Drew Gooden and a tough, veteran backcourt in Kirk Hinrich and Jeff Boschee.

Like Maryland, Kansas liked to play at a fast pace and had enough capable players on the bench to do it. The Jayhawks, the first team to go undefeated in the Big 12 Conference regular season, were 33–3 overall and led the nation in scoring, averaging ninety-one points per game. They were a formidable opponent.

"They resemble us and we resemble them, however you want to say it," Boschee said. "They've got all the weapons, just like us. I think the game is going to be won by who wants it more."

Despite Boschee's analysis, it was impossible to believe that at this point in the season one team's players could possibly "want it more" than the other's.

Rather, the key would be which team's top players delivered.

• • •

If the Terrapins needed any reminder that they would have to play at their best to advance to the finals, it came in the night's first game, when Indiana stunned heavily favored Oklahoma, 73–64.

The game, though, started about as poorly as it could for the Terrapins. Wilcox missed a quick jumper, then committed a turnover. Passes by Byron Mouton and Steve Blake were off the mark and Lonny Baxter was called for a charge, giving Maryland turnovers on four consecutive possessions.

The only positive was that Wilcox clearly had come to play. On Kansas's first possession, Wilcox blocked a jumper in the lane by Gooden. The Jayhawks' next shot, a fast-break drive by Gooden, was swatted away by the menacing Maryland forward. Just as he had been against Illinois and Duke, Wilcox was ready when it mattered most.

Blake finally got the Terrapins on the board with a fast-break layup, but six seconds later Baxter was called for his second foul, getting guard Aaron Miles on a shot. With 17:19 left in the half, Maryland's starting center went to the bench. Then Dixon missed from an impossible angle under the backboard, and Tahj Holden, in the game for Baxter, missed a three-pointer from the top of key.

Off the miss, Kansas got out on the break and Hinrich buried an open three-pointer from the right wing for a 10–2 lead. Gary Williams called a timeout, pointing to his temples as if to scream, "*Think!*" But Dixon missed a three-point try, and after Gooden saved the ball from going out of bounds, Boschee delivered a three-pointer from the left wing. The Jayhawks led 13–2 at the first television timeout, and Williams went off on his players.

"Gary said we were all pussies," Wilcox explained later. "And he wanted us to try to prove him wrong."

Off the inbounds play, Drew Nicholas fed Wilcox for a dunk. A minute later, Wilcox found Dixon for a three-pointer from the left corner. Slowly, Maryland crept back into the game, with Kansas's three-point shooters going cold and Wilcox doing a number on Gooden inside, with help from Holden and Ryan Randle.

With seven and a half minutes left in the half, Dixon pulled up on a fast break and nailed a three-pointer from the right wing to give Maryland its first lead, 26–25. The Jayhawks knew they had to watch Dixon, but they still could not stop him. He was fouled on a three-point try and made two of three free throws, then made a three-pointer from the right wing after Kansas went into a 2–3 zone defense. Later, Dixon drew the defense on a pick-and-roll and fed Wilcox for a three-point play, helping the Terrapins take a 44–37 halftime lead.

"I just took it upon myself to try to hit some big shots," Dixon said. "I helped my team get back in the game."

As they went to the locker room, Maryland's players knew they had taken the Jayhawks' punch and responded with their own combination, rallying from an eleven-point deficit. And all this had occurred even though Baxter played just forty-one seconds after getting his second foul.

The second half started with yet another electric dunk by Wilcox, but Maryland couldn't shake Kansas. A pair of three-pointers by Boschee—the first ending a stretch of twenty minutes without a three-pointer for the Jayhawks—cut Maryland's lead to 60–55 with twelve minutes left.

Just as they had done for the past two months, though, the Terrapins found a way to kick their game to another level. This time Blake led the team's surge, temporarily breaking out of his slump. After sitting out several minutes with three fouls, he reentered the game and immediately made an offensive impact.

Blake made an open three-pointer from the left wing, then fed Dixon for a jumper from the foul line. After a miss by the struggling Gooden, who could not adjust to being guarded by the taller, athletic Wilcox, Blake pushed the ball up the court and fed Holden for a three-point play. Back on defense, Blake took a charge—the fourth foul on Hinrich—and at the other end Holden banked in a running shot.

In less than two minutes, Maryland had scored ten consecutive points. It was 70–55, and Kansas was in danger of being blown out.

A few minutes later, Blake penetrated and then passed to Dixon for a three-pointer from the left corner, and it was 83–63 with six minutes left. Terrapin fans all over, from those lucky enough to be in the Georgia Dome to those who had assembled to watch the game on video screens in Cole Field House, knew the championship game was within reach.

Knowing their team's history, though, perhaps they should have known better. No longer running any effective offense, Maryland was missing shots and making turnovers, and went nearly five minutes without a basket. And Kansas took advantage, pulling within five points, 87–82, on a three-pointer from the left wing by Boschee with 2:03 left.

The Terrapins had the lead, but the Jayhawks had all the momentum.

Maryland fans had grown used to heartbreak over the years, seeing their team come oh-so-close without ever being able to finish. In particular, the losses to Duke the previous season sprang to mind. Terrapin fans were jaded to the point that most thought every blue sky had storm clouds waiting to move in.

Dixon once again tried to assert himself, but missed a quick three-pointer from the left corner. Kansas could cut the lead to three points or, with a three-pointer, even two. Maryland was in jeopardy of perhaps the most agonizing loss in school history. The Terrapins had blown a twenty-two-point lead against Duke in the previous season's Final Four, but at least that lead was in the first half. This time, the lead was twenty points with only six minutes left in the game.

With a chance to make it a one-possession game, though, Miles was called for traveling. With the ball back in his hands, Dixon wasn't going to miss again. He sank a ten-foot runner from along the left baseline to make it 89–82 with 1:12 left. It was the Terrapins' only field goal in the final six minutes, but it was all they would need.

Boschee countered with a three, Dixon made two free throws, and Gooden made a three-pointer to make it 92–88 with 19.8 seconds left. Kansas still had a chance, though it disappeared before the clock moved another tenth of a second. Jayhawk players signaled for a timeout as soon as Gooden's shot went in—but Kansas was out of timeouts, so a technical foul was called. Maryland made five of six free throws in the closing seconds, securing a date in Monday night's championship game with a 97–88 victory.

Dixon had made ten of eighteen shots and matched his career high with thirty-three points. "Just another Juan Dixon NCAA tournament game," Nicholas said. "He keeps on getting better. The deeper we go, the better he gets. He just finds a way to do it."

Baxter had had just four points in fourteen minutes, but Wilcox had come through with eighteen points and nine rebounds. And the bench had been particularly vital. Holden had thirteen points, and while Randle had just two points and two rebounds, he also had two blocks and was effective in fifteen minutes. It was a long way from the beginning of the season, when Williams had not trusted Randle on the court in key situations. Randle, who had come to Maryland so out of shape that he had vomited in his first workout with strength-and-conditioning coach Kurtis Shultz, hadn't even gotten in the season opener against Arizona or the loss at Oklahoma and had played only one minute in the ACC opener at N.C. State.

By the time the postseason rolled around, Randle was getting quality playing time. Still, he hardly looked like he belonged—just about every time he made a play, it seemed, Randle would smile or become giddy, as if he couldn't believe he was doing such things at this level.

"When he came in, I thought he was fat," Williams said. "I said, 'Man, you've got to get in shape. You think you can play here in that shape?' He does a double take and he's like, 'Man, who's this?' Then you get to know each other and it's good. It's amazing how it changes in twelve months."

• • •

Twelve months earlier, the Maryland Terrapins had been reeling from a devastating defeat. Now they were preparing for the biggest game in their lives and the school's history.

The next two days seemed to take forever. Because CBS wanted the game in prime time, the championship game would not tip off until after 9 P.M., giving the players plenty of time to think ahead and red-clad fans plenty of time to enjoy Atlanta.

For Maryland, this was the moment it had been waiting for all season—actually since the 2000–01 season had ended with the semifinal loss to Duke. The Terrapins were forty minutes from achieving their goal, and they were an eight-point favorite.

"This is a big game for us," Juan Dixon said. "I have a chance to be a part of something unbelievable."

The game's key matchup was going to be Dixon against Indiana's Dane Fife, the Big Ten Conference's co–defensive player of the year. Fife was slightly taller than Dixon and thirty-five pounds heavier, but Dixon—who had had trouble during the regular season when guarded by some bigger opponents—pledged that size would not be a factor.

"I'm not worried at all," Dixon said. "I'm just going to go out and play my game. I'm not talking trash, but that's just the type of person I am. I have a lot of confidence in my ability. They can try to double-team me, box-and-one me. I don't think it's going to work.

"I might be small, but I ain't weak. I'm not going to let any guys push up on me. I ain't a dirty player, but I might throw a few cheap shots here and there."

While Maryland (31–4) had been pointing to this game since before the start of the season, Indiana (24–11) was trying to tie the record for most losses by a champion. The Hoosiers were a true underdog, but they had Maryland's attention, having defeated Duke and Oklahoma, two of the teams that had beaten the Terrapins during the regular season.

"I can promise you that we are not going to underestimate Indiana at all," Dixon said.

• • •

Perhaps the thing Maryland's players underestimated was their nerves. They had played in big games, but this one was different. This was the game that would determine their place in history. In the locker room before the game, Dixon broke down in tears, insisting the team find a way to win.

Blake started the game with a bad pass for a turnover, one of four turnovers by the Terrapins in the opening three minutes. Indiana wasn't much better, making one of its first seven shots and turning the ball over three times.

Dixon, though, got Maryland going. Byron Mouton passed to Dixon for a three-pointer from the left corner, and then Blake rebounded an Indiana miss, dribbled up the court, and passed to Dixon for a long jumper from the left wing. Soon Baxter scored with his standard right-handed move and Dixon made two free throws. Then Baxter made a put-back—continuing a trend that saw Maryland get every loose ball—and Dixon made a steal and a layup.

It was 19–8 midway through the half, and the Terrapins seemed on their way, with Dixon scoring at a point-per-minute clip.

"Your best player, if you are going to win a championship, has to step up and make plays," Indiana coach Mike Davis said. "And he did that. He got them off to a great start."

The Hoosiers, though, were plenty resilient, having rallied from a seventeen-point deficit to stun Duke earlier in the tournament.

Point guard Tom Coverdale, playing on an injured ankle, made a pair of three-pointers. Guard Kyle Hornsby made a jumper and a three-pointer. And when Coverdale weaved down the lane and made a bank shot to close the half, Maryland's lead was a tenuous 31–25. Worse, Dixon had cooled off, not even attempting a shot in the final ten minutes. Baxter had made just three of ten shots. The team had ten turnovers and had shot only four free throws, an indication of a lack of aggressive play.

The sloppiness continued in the second half. The Terrapins led by single digits until an Indiana tip-in by backup center and Atlanta native Jeff Newton tied it, 40–40, with 11:43 left. Williams called a timeout.

After the timeout, Dixon fed Baxter for a post-up bank shot—as always, to the right; Baxter was fouled on the play, but he missed the free throws. Jared Jeffries, the Big Ten player of the year, scored for Indiana to tie it at 42–42, and then Baxter uncharacteristically missed a pair of free throws. And when Wilcox was called for goaltending on a layup by Jeffries, Indiana had its first lead of the night, 44–42.

Hooiser fans throughout the huge Georgia Dome were going crazy. Would this game provide the final story line for "Hoosiers II," as several Indiana players had called their postseason run?

The skinny guy wearing number 3 in a white uniform had other ideas, and he made certain that that was the only time Indiana led.

Eleven seconds after the Jeffries basket, Blake beat the press and passed out to Dixon for a three-pointer from the left side, which put Maryland back in front, 45–44.

"Not every big scorer wants to take those shots," Williams said. "But Juan has never backed away from a shot in that situation."

Fife badly missed a three-point try. Dixon fed Baxter, who was fouled and made both free throws. Fife answered with a jumper from the left corner of the foul line. But then Dixon made one of the greatest shots of his career.

With Indiana trying to stay close, Dixon dribbled to his left and went up for a seventeen-foot jumper from the left side. Fife was with him step for step and it appeared he might block the shot. Dixon, though, hung in the air an extra second before releasing the ball. It was 49–46, and while Dixon's basket was only two points, it might as well have been ten.

Maryland scored fifteen of the next eighteen points, and soon the only thing left to do was run out the clock.

As the final seconds elapsed, Gary Williams was in disbelief.

"You keep checking the time to make sure the score and time is right, that you're really going to win," he said.

In just a few short seconds, dozens of images flashed through Williams's mind. He thought about many of the players to come through the program, especially Walt Williams, the star player who had chosen not to transfer when the NCAA handed down its sanctions in 1990.

Time finally ran out. Juan Dixon hurled the ball in the air, then hugged Holden; quickly Baxter toppled him to the court, and the two seniors, the team's leaders, embraced.

They had done it.

• • •

In the ensuing on-court celebration, Maryland cut down the nets, received the championship plaque, and watched the commemorative video. It was sheer euphoria for a team that had finally achieved the goal it had set for itself so long ago.

"At one point, I was so happy that I couldn't get the tears out of my own eyes," Drew Nicholas said, delivering perhaps the best line of the night. "I don't know if you guys have ever felt that, but I hope you do someday. There is no way to describe it."

Amid all the celebrating, though, Gary Williams still had one thing on his mind.

The previous weekend, after beating Connecticut to advance to the Final Four, the players had doused Williams with water and juice drinks as soon as they got into the locker room. The drenched coach had been forced to take off his suit and don backup point guard Andre Collins's warm-ups for the postgame news conference and interviews and the trip home.

Before the Final Four weekend started, Williams had promised that if his team won it all, he would go to the ESPN Zone in the trendy Buckhead area of Atlanta to appear on the *SportsCenter* set after the championship game. And he didn't want to look like crap. So as the players celebrated their triumph, Williams sought out the closest thing Maryland had to a bodyguard, the burly Kurtis Shultz.

"You need to be right next to me and I cannot have water poured on me," Williams told Shultz, figuring the strength coach's presence would scare off the revelers. "I cannot get wet. Make sure you stand in front of me."

Shultz was not about to take any chances, though, and ordered the team managers to go to the locker room and get rid of all the water and other beverages. The players had just given their all for forty minutes and exulted on the court for an hour, but if they were thirsty, they would have to wait.

After a postgame news conference and a few interviews in the locker room, the players headed back to the Hilton Hotel near the airport, about fifteen minutes to the south. Williams had to go to Buckhead, about twenty minutes to the north. ESPN had arranged for transportation for Williams from the Georgia Dome. Expecting a luxury ride, Williams was surprised when he and Kevin Messenger were led to a white passenger van.

"I guess all the limos were taken," Williams said, laughing as he remembered the empty fast-food wrappers that littered the van's floor.

The bottles of Dom Perignon must have been taken, too. Instead, there was a six-pack of Amstel Light on ice in a plastic punch bowl that apparently had been taken from one of the dome's hospitality rooms.

"It tasted pretty good at the time," said Williams, who would have preferred a Bud Light.

On the air, Williams teased Dick Vitale, who was wearing a Maryland hat. "What happened to your Duke hat?" he said, prompting Vitale to throw the Maryland cap at Williams.

It was a night for fun, jokes, and partying. Williams could not believe the mob scene when he arrived back at the team hotel around 2 A.M.

"You forget that everybody knew where we were staying," he said.

It would be another sleepless night for the coach, who had had many throughout his career. But this one was different: CBS had booked the coach of the national championship team for a 7 A.M. interview on its morning show. After working so long to get to this point, how could Williams refuse?

EPILOGUE

"Wow"

As soon as time expired in the championship game, Juan Dixon hurled the ball in the air.

Before it had reached its peak high above the Georgia Dome court, Steve Blake had his eyes on the ball. Blake was used to dishing out passes—in his three seasons he had already set the school record for assists—but on this occasion, he wanted to be the one on the receiving end. So while his teammates hugged and photographers rushed onto the court to capture every moment, Blake focused on the ball. He wanted one last keepsake from Maryland's magical run to its first national title.

Blake knew, after all, that once that ball came down, everything would be different for the Terrapins.

Juan Dixon, Lonny Baxter, and Byron Mouton had completed their eligibility and would join new teams—professional teams.

A few weeks later, Chris Wilcox, the precocious sophomore forward, announced that he, too, would be joining the professional ranks.

Gary Williams had hoped that Wilcox would return for one more season in order to gain experience and benefit from the chance to be one of the team's primary offensive threats. The money, though, was too much to pass up. Wilcox's departure was not a surprise.

"I knew the whole time that if he ever had a coming-out party in his first two years at Maryland, he was going to be in the NBA the following year," assistant coach Dave Dickerson said. "He's that kind of player. A good game with him or a great game with him is the type of game no one else on our team could have. You don't see that shit. Len Bias is the only other player I saw if he went crazy in a game, he was on another level. He wasn't on the same playing field. Chris Wilcox has the same qualities."

Seeing the other four starters depart, Steve Blake gave consideration to skipping his senior season.

Nor was it simply his NBA-bound Maryland teammates who fed his thoughts of turning pro. In the summer of 2000, Blake had played on a national junior team along with Jason Williams of Duke, Jason Richardson of Michigan State, Drew Gooden of Kansas, Tayshaun Prince of Kentucky, and Joe Johnson of Arkansas. Another national team that Blake played on, in high school, included Florida's Mike Miller, Missouri's Keyon Dooling, and Quentin Richardson and Bobby Simmons of DePaul. All of those players were either already in the NBA or on their way this summer.

"I hold my own against those guys," Blake said. "That starts to help you. I thought about it a little bit. But I just figured it was best if I have one more good year, I have a chance to move way up in the draft. I just didn't have a good tournament and I think that hurt me a lot. But I'm not complaining, because we won the whole thing. Everything worked out."

While he would not have the company of his fellow starters, Blake had a nice keepsake in the ball from the championship game. He had the rest of the team sign it, but was unsure where he might put it.

"It's on the floor right now," Blake said during the summer. "I haven't gotten a case for it yet. I'll get something. I see it every day."

• • •

If Steve Blake was the sole returning starter for the 2002–03 season, at least he knew that the team's entire coaching staff also would be returning to College Park.

After Maryland won the championship, assistant coach Jimmy Patsos had received some interest from Boise State University during its coaching search, but he would be coming back to Maryland in 2002–03.

Dave Dickerson had had to make a wrenching decision, passing up the head coaching opportunity he had longed for.

While the team returned on a charter flight to College Park the morning after beating Indiana, Dickerson had traveled to Charleston, South Carolina, to interview for the coaching position at the College of Charleston. Before he got to Charleston, he thought this would be the perfect opportunity.

"Thank God for interviews," Dickerson said. "It just wasn't a great situation. I was more disappointed for my wife and my family in South Carolina, but I knew I couldn't take that job. I think that staying at Maryland would have been better.

"The main thing that was going through my mind was that my job got better two nights before [when the team won the national championship]. I had to compare my job now to that job then. I just felt that Maryland was a much better situation for me than going down there as a head coach."

A few nights later, Dickerson called Charleston athletic director Jerry Baker. He was pulling out of the process.

"For the first time in my life since being associated with the University of Maryland, I felt my decision to come to Maryland was right," Dickerson said. "I encountered the Len Bias tragedy, being here as a student-athlete when the school and athletic department was at its lowest point. When we went to the Final Four last year and won the national championship this year, it just reaffirmed that I made the right decision to come here as a high school student back in eighty-whatever-it-was.

"I became a good student here and graduated with my degree, but there was still a part of me that felt I had made a bad decision to come here. Because my basketball life was a roller coaster. And I felt that I didn't enjoy my basketball life here, being an athlete. It wasn't because of anything I did. Just timing. Len Bias. Lefty resigning. Bob Wade and that was it. There was nothing to look forward to. Nothing to talk about. I played on two good teams, my freshman year and my junior year, but something happened to both of those teams that made those seasons look obsolete.

"My coaching career at Maryland has been like reliving my basketball career. I feel like one of the guys really, because that's what I'm using to substitute for my four years of playing here."

● ● ●

In the days, weeks, and months after the victory over Indiana, the Maryland team was showered with honors.

Immediately after the title game, Gary Williams had to deal with a deluge of congratulatory phone calls and letters. President George W. Bush and Vice President Dick Cheney were among the many who sent letters of congratulations. Williams also found that former teammates, former players, fellow coaches, and acquaintances all wanted to drop a line to the man who only thirteen months before had been regarded as one of the best coaches never to make it to the Final Four. Now he had two Final Four appearances and a national championship on his résumé.

Among those calling to offer congratulations was legendary Baltimore Colts quarterback Johnny Unitas.

"It was neat to get to know him," Williams said. "He called after the final and said, 'Williams, that's like when we beat the Giants.'

"That's kind of impressive when somebody like that takes the time to make a call like that and then says that. I told him he still isn't getting any more strokes" on the golf course. (Unfortunately, the two did not have long to nurture their friendship, as Unitas passed away just five months later.)

There were rallies for the Terrapins in Baltimore and Cole Field House. The Maryland legislature honored the team in Annapolis, and the state's congressional delegation welcomed the Terrapins on the U.S. Capitol grounds. Finally, in mid-May, the team was invited to the White House, where it joined three other national champions—the University of Connecticut women's basketball team, the University of Minnesota men's hockey team, and the University of Minnesota–Duluth women's hockey team. In a ceremony on the South Lawn, Juan Dixon and Lonny Baxter presented President Bush with a number 1 Maryland jersey.

"You guys showed some things that are important for our country, particularly at this time," Bush told the teams. "You showed something greater than yourself, called a team, can achieve great things. You recognize that some things in life are worth more than just an individual record and you recognize there is something bigger than an individual accomplishment."

Bush was speaking to the four teams, but his words were especially true for the Maryland Terrapins.

• • •

Inevitably, though, the players would have to go their separate ways.

At the NBA draft in late June, the nineteen-year-old Wilcox became the first Terrapin selected, when he was chosen eighth overall by the Los Angeles Clippers. Wilcox might have been raw and young, but he had that freakish athleticism that was too difficult to pass up.

About one hour later, Dixon was taken seventeenth overall by the Washington Wizards. He had not been invited to the NBA draft party at Madison Square Garden in New York, but Dixon attended the event on his own. A few minutes after being selected, he began crying while talking on a cell phone to his brother, Phil, who was hosting a draft-watching party at home in Baltimore. Dixon's determination had paid off: the mock draft he had posted on his bedroom wall months before had had him being selected in the middle of the second round, and here he was, a first-round NBA draft pick.

Midway through the second round, Lonny Baxter was selected by the Chicago Bulls, the forty-fourth pick overall.

Byron Mouton was not drafted. He played for the Washington Wizards team in a summer league and attended the Boston Celtics' training camp before being one of the last players cut. He then signed a contract with the Idaho Stampede of the Continental Basketball Association.

• • •

Although the congratulatory letters and phone calls slowed down, Gary Williams did not get much of a break. Through the summer he had a long list of public appearances and speaking engagements. Some were part of his annual off-season program. Others came along with the responsibility of being a national champion.

Williams was tired from the longest season in school history, one that began with its earliest season opener and ended with its first national championship. But he knew that he could not disappoint people who wanted to hear what it was like to be a champion.

"It was great," Williams said. "Sometimes you daydream about what it might be like, then you do it and everything hits so quick. Whoever wins the national championship gets to do this and that. It's very time-consuming. I really value my time after the season is over, and that was taken away from me. But at the same time, you want to experience everything.

"I think when you coach, you don't get the chance to stop and look at the history of things or whatever. This year, I've probably done it more than any other because I get asked about it all the time. It doesn't sink in, you just keep moving. You think about it and there are times you realize what you did, but you don't sit around and think, 'Wow, we won the national championship.' You realize the magnitude every once in a while. But it just comes up. It's never planned."

APPENDIX

2001–02 Season Statistics

En route to the national championship, the Maryland Terrapins racked up some impressive numbers, as shown in the pages that follow. Individuals also were recognized for their achievements during the season: Juan Dixon was a first-team All-American, the ACC player of the year, and the Final Four's most outstanding player. Lonny Baxter was named second-team All-ACC and an honorable mention All-American. Steve Blake was selected to the All-ACC third team and joined Baxter as an honorable mention All-American. Chris Wilcox, who became a lottery pick in the June 2002 NBA draft, also earned third-team All-ACC honors. Byron Mouton was an honorable mention All-ACC selection. Gary Williams was named ACC coach of the year and *Basketball America*'s national coach of the year.

In all, it was a historic season for Maryland basketball.

Overall Record: 32–4

Date		Opponent	W/L	Score
11/08/01	*vs.*	Arizona*	L	67–71
11/09/01	*vs.*	Temple*	W	82–74
11/17/01		American	W	83–53
11/24/01		Delaware State	W	77–53
11/27/01		Illinois	W	76–63
12/02/01	*vs.*	Princeton†	W	61–53
12/03/01	*vs.*	Connecticut†	W	77–65
12/09/01		Detroit	W	79–54
12/11/01		Monmouth	W	91–55
12/21/01	*at*	Oklahoma	L	56–72
12/27/01		William & Mary	W	103–75
12/30/01	*at*	North Carolina State	W	72–65
01/03/02		Norfolk State	W	92–69
01/09/02		North Carolina	W	112–79
01/13/02	*at*	Georgia Tech	W	92–87
01/17/02	*at*	Duke	L	78–99
01/20/02		Clemson	W	99–90
01/23/02	*at*	Wake Forest	W	85–63
01/26/02		Florida State	W	84–63
01/31/02	*at*	Virginia	W	91–87
02/03/02		North Carolina State	W	89–73
02/10/02	*at*	North Carolina	W	92–77
02/13/02		Georgia Tech	W	85–65
02/17/02		Duke	W	87–73
02/20/02	*at*	Clemson	W	84–68
02/24/02		Wake Forest	W	90–89
02/27/02	*at*	Florida State	W	96–63
03/03/02		Virginia	W	112–92
ACC TOURNAMENT				
03/08/02	*vs.*	Florida State‡	W	85–59
03/09/02	*vs.*	North Carolina State‡	L	82–86
NCAA TOURNAMENT				
03/15/02	*vs.*	Siena College§	W	85–70
03/17/02	*vs.*	University of Wisconsin§	W	87–57
03/22/02	*vs.*	Kentucky**	W	78–68
03/24/02	*vs.*	Connecticut**	W	90–82
03/30/02	*vs.*	Kansas††	W	97–88
04/01/02	*vs.*	Indiana††	W	64–52

* At Madison Square Garden, New York, New York (Coaches vs. Cancer Classic)

† At MCI Center, Washington, D.C. (BB&T Classic)

‡ At Charlotte Coliseum, Charlotte, North Carolina

§ At MCI Center, Washington, D.C. (NCAA First and Second Rounds)

** At Carrier Dome, Syracuse, New York (NCAA East Regional)

†† At Georgia Dome, Atlanta, Georgia (NCAA Final Four)

Team Statistics

	Maryland	Opponent
SCORING	3060	2552
Points per game	85.0	70.9
Scoring margin	+14.1	—
FIELD GOALS—ATT	1083–2248	920–2304
Field goal pct.	.482	.399
3-POINT FG—ATT	217–580	227–717
3-point FG pct.	.374	.317
3-pt FG made per game	6.0	6.3
FREE THROWS—ATT	677–933	485–712
Free throw pct.	.726	.681
REBOUNDS	1479	1347
Rebounds per game	41.1	37.4
Rebounding margin	+3.7	—
ASSISTS	714	489
Assists per game	19.8	13.6
TURNOVERS	495	555
Turnovers per game	13.8	15.4
Turnover margin	+1.7	—
Assist/turnover ratio	1.4	0.9
STEALS	302	256
Steals per game	8.4	7.1
BLOCKS	216	128
Blocks per game	6.0	3.6
WINNING STREAK	6	—
Home win streak	15	—

Individual Statistics

#	Player	GP–GS	Min	FG%	3PT%	FT%	R/G	A/G	Stl	Blk	Pts/G
03	Dixon, Juan	36–36	33.6	.469	.397	.898	4.6	2.9	92	7	20.4
35	Baxter, Lonny	35–35	28.7	.545	.000	.623	8.2	0.8	33	69	15.2
54	Wilcox, Chris	36–26	24.1	.504	.000	.585	7.1	1.5	28	53	12.0
01	Mouton, Byron	36–35	28.3	.469	.255	.767	5.0	2.1	34	6	11.1
25	Blake, Steve	36–36	32.0	.382	.344	.824	3.8	7.9	56	16	8.0
12	Nicholas, Drew	36–1	20.5	.477	.396	.803	2.3	2.4	16	12	7.1
45	Holden, Tahj	36–11	18.5	.453	.425	.836	2.7	1.2	21	34	5.6
33	Randle, Ryan	34–0	9.6	.524	1.000	.563	3.1	0.1	13	18	3.8
10	Collins, Andre	22–0	3.8	.667	.500	.778	0.5	0.9	5	0	2.2
05	McCall, Calvin	19–0	4.2	.526	.500	.500	0.8	0.1	3	1	1.4
21	Grinnon, Mike	16–0	2.1	.286	.250	1.000	0.3	0.3	1	0	0.4
04	Badu, Earl	12–0	2.2	.500	.000	.000	0.3	0.8	0	0	0.3

ACKNOWLEDGMENTS

The idea for this book first arose during the 2001 NCAA tournament, when several colleagues asked if I was thinking about taking on a project if Maryland were to win the national title.

It was on hold for a year after the Terrapins lost to Duke in the Final Four, but in 2002, with the team making another postseason run, the inquiries were even more frequent. Ken Denlinger, one of the most respected writers in the business and an accomplished author, was kind enough to put me in touch with his agent, Faith Hamlin, and she began exploring the possibilities.

Among those who wanted to know if the project would happen was Dick Weiss of the *New York Daily News.* "You've got to do it," Hoops, as he is known to everyone, said after Maryland's championship victory over Indiana.

That night, having packed my bags to catch a 6 A.M. flight back to Washington, I went to the team hotel near the airport. I wanted to survey the scene and let the team's publicist, Kevin Messenger, know that his assistance might be needed. A friend, Dan Rochkind—who during my first years on the beat broadcast games on the campus radio station,

WMUC—overheard the conversation. Dan is friends with Alex Novak, the marketing director for Regnery Publishing, and soon Dan introduced me to the son of noted Maryland fan and political commentator Bob Novak.

We chatted for a few minutes, and the next day Alex sent me an e-mail. That's how the deal got started.

There are dozens of other people who helped make this happen and countless others who have shaped my writing and reporting over the years.

Faith Hamlin worked wonders via the phone, e-mail, and FedEx.

Thanks also go to the folks at Regnery, including publisher Al Regnery. My editor, Jed Donahue, a Georgetown University alum and dedicated Hoya fan, was wonderful to work with.

My boss at the *Washington Post,* George Solomon, has been tremendously supportive of my career, and I'd like to thank him and the other editors for allowing me to take on this project. Many of the stories in this book came from articles I wrote during the season and my previous time on the beat.

Several colleagues have gone out of their way to lend their knowledge over the years, including Mark Asher, Richard Justice, Dave Sell, Liz Clarke, Bill Gildea, Rachel Nichols, Len Shapiro, Jim Brady, and Michael Wilbon, my traveling companion four weekends each March. I deeply appreciate the help of Russell James and Kim Oster of the Washington Post Writer's Group, who helped secure photographs from throughout the season. Bill Vaughan also was kind enough to let me look at a trove of his terrific photographs, some of which are included in this book.

A handful of friends with knowledge of Maryland and college basketball eagerly—at least that's what they said—read unedited sections so I would not omit any pertinent details or anecdotes: David Ginsburg, Mark Thomas, and Steve Argeris. Their suggestions and advice were invaluable.

Thanks also go to the writers in other cities who supplied wonderful anecdotes throughout the season.

Perhaps most important in my career, I have been extremely fortunate to work for people who cared about their job and were willing to pass on their wisdom. Among others, this goes for Ed Laubach and Barry Miller of the *Express-Times* in Easton, Pennsylvania, and Scott Briscoe when we worked together at the *Journal Messenger* in Manassas, Virginia. Neil Greenberger, the noted softball coach, hired me at the *Post,* giving me the honor of taking Friday-night high school box scores. Steve Berkowitz provided me the opportunity to cover Naval Academy football and subsequently University of Maryland football and basketball. Matt Rennie now has the misfortune of listening to my daily travails and makes things easy.

At Maryland, Messenger answered plenty of ticky-tack questions and helped arrange interviews. I am deeply grateful to Gary Williams and his players and coaching staff for giving so much of their time and insight, both during the season and looking back. They talked openly about a variety of subjects, including several I'm sure they would have preferred to avoid. Many of these interviews were used to re-create scenes that occurred over the past few years.

Thanks also go to Cleo Long-Thomas and Carole Bucco, who couldn't hide their excitement every time I called for Gary or one of his assistants. Pat Shannon went the extra mile to lend videotapes of games from throughout the season.

Family and friends were kind enough not to mind while I fell off the radar and skipped family dinners. Thanks to Mom, Dad, and Robin. There were too many nights when I tucked Jodi in and went back to the makeshift office in the dining room.

If I left anybody out, I truly am sorry. This has been one of the hardest parts of the book to write.

INDEX

PHOTO CREDITS

Dust jacket photos
Front cover: Bill Vaughan/Icon SMI.
Front cover: Dave Martin/AP Wide World Photos.

Photo insert
Page 1, top: © 2002, *Washington Post* photo by Jonathan Newton. Reprinted with permission.
Page 1, bottom: Maryland Media Relations.
Page 2, top: © 2002, *Washington Post* photo by Jonathan Newton. Reprinted with permission.
Page 2, bottom: © 2002, *Washington Post* photo by Jonathan Newton. Reprinted with permission.
Page 3, top: © 2002, *Washington Post* photo by Jonathan Newton. Reprinted with permission.
Page 3, bottom: © 2002, *Washington Post* photo by John McDonnell. Reprinted with permission.
Page 4, top: © 2002, *Washington Post* photo by Kevin Clark. Reprinted with permission.
Page 4, bottom: © 2002, *Washington Post* photo by Joel Richardson. Reprinted with permission.
Page 5, top left: © 2002, *Washington Post* photo by Jonathan Newton. Reprinted with permission.
Page 5, top right: © 2002, *Washington Post* photo by John McDonnell. Reprinted with permission.
Page 5, bottom: © 2002, *Washington Post* photo by John McDonnell. Reprinted with permission.
Page 6, top: © 2002, *Washington Post* photo by Jonathan Newton. Reprinted with permission.
Page 6, bottom left: Bill Vaughan.
Page 6, bottom right: Bill Vaughan.
Page 7, top: © 2002, *Washington Post* photo by Jonathan Newton. Reprinted with permission.
Page 7, bottom: © 2002, *Washington Post* photo by Kevin Clark. Reprinted with permission.
Page 8, top: © 2002, *Washington Post* photo by John McDonnell. Reprinted with permission.
Page 8, bottom left: Bill Vaughan.
Page 8, bottom right: © 2002, *Washington Post* photo by Michael Williamson. Reprinted with permission.